Insider Guide

Careers in Accounting

2005 Edition

WetFeet ®

Helping you make smarter career decisions.

8-11-05

WetFeet, Inc.

The Folger Building
101 Howard Street
Suite 300
San Francisco, CA 94105

Phone: (415) 284-7900 or 1-800-926-4JOB
Fax: (415) 284-7910
Website: www.WetFeet.com

Careers In Accounting

ISBN: 1-58207-451-8

Table of Contents

Accounting at a Glance

Opportunity Overview

The accounting industry has been through some difficult times in recent years, as all major accounting firms have been implicated in scandals, and accounting-rule changes have added work to the plates of public accounting firms and industry finance departments alike. One major firm, Arthur Andersen, was forced out of the picture as a result, turning the Big Five into the Big Four. But with the business environment stronger than it's been in several years, there are opportunities for entry-level and midcareer types in both public accounting and management accounting.

- Most industry hires are recent graduates of college or university accounting programs.

- By far, the most hires are for audit positions; some hires are also brought into tax practices.

- Big Four accounting careers offer a predictable career path and great experience should you decide to leave Big Four accounting.

Major Pluses about Careers in Accounting

- The Big Four and other firms give employees exposure to a wide range of companies and industries and a lot of responsibility. Thus employees develop impressive skill sets that they can take elsewhere, whether they want to hang out their own accounting shingle, go into industry finance, or pursue an entirely different profession.

- You'll use top-flight technology if you go to work in the Big Four. These firms have been among the most savvy and aggressive users of intranets, extranets, and e-commerce technologies.

- In good times and bad, corporations and other institutions need accountants, and it remains *de rigueur* for Fortune 500 companies to use the Big Four for accounting services.

Major Minuses about Accounting Careers

- There can be quite a bit of internal politics in Big Four and other big firms when it comes to staffing.

- Bureaucracy central: Accounting involves myriad rules, regulations, reviews, and checklists, and some insiders complain that a feeling of administration overload often creeps unnecessarily into other aspects of their professional lives.

- Accountants are notorious for working late, especially during tax season. There are always client demands to be met and numbers to be checked—and double-checked.

Recruiting Overview

The good news here is that accounting firms are hiring. Between things like new accounting rules and increasing mergers and acquisitions activity, public accountancies are staffing up. Because of these things and a few others, management accountants, who work in-house for companies of all kinds, are also finding increasing opportunities.

The Big Four and many second-tier firms recruit on college campuses across the country. (Other second tier firms may recruit regionally.) At schools that are a recruiting focus for a particular firm, the process begins with a campus presentation by representatives of the firm. The interviewing process begins with first-round on-campus interviews. After the initial round of interviews, recruiters will choose candidates to be called back for second-round interviews. Some firms conduct one or two big office interviewing days for the second round; others spread out the office visits.

Students at schools where the firms of their choice don't have a presence—including candidates interested in smaller public accounting firms—and mid-career candidates should contact the firms directly. Remember: The best way to make this M.O. work is to network and find a personal contact within the firm of your choice.

Accounting firms look for the following skills and attributes:

- Analytical ability

- Leadership

- Written and oral communication skills

- Attention to detail

- Ability to work independently

- Team skills

- Work ethic

- High ethical standards

- Computer literacy

The Industry

- Overview
- The Bottom Line
- How It Breaks Down
- Industry Trends
- Industry Rankings

Overview

When thinking about the accounting industry, most folks conjure up images of solitary bean counters, their backs hunched and brows furrowed in concentration as they pore over accounting ledgers. "Ever changing" and "quickly evolving" are not the kinds of phrases that immediately come to mind. But in the past 10 or 12 years, this industry has undergone not just one, but several massive upheavals against a backdrop of constant industry consolidation.

It used to be that the group of the biggest public accounting firms was known as the Big Eight. Their main business focus was auditing public companies. Relative to other industries, accounting was a nice, steady industry, with modest but predictable profits. Accounting firms had a reputation for humility, discretion, and high ethics.

During the early days of the tech boom in the early 1990s, though, the major accounting firms started making enormous profits from IT consulting work (while taking their auditing work for granted). People in the industry stopped looking at auditing as their bread and butter and began looking at auditing as a way to build relationships that might lead to much more profitable consulting engagements. Accounting firms had no problem with the conflicts of interest implicit in trying to independently verify their clients' financial statements while relying on those same clients for massive IT contracts. Eventually, the big accountancies got out of consulting for reasons that include regulatory pressure and a softening consulting market. It was too late, though; the accountancies had made all kinds of egregious errors in judgment—and broken the law—in pursuit of consulting windfalls from audit clients. When they were caught, the major accounting firms were battered by a maelstrom of bad press that continues to this day.

Today, thanks to industry consolidation and the collapse of Arthur Andersen due to the misdeeds of Arthur Andersen accountants working on Enron's books, the Big Eight has become the Big Four: Deloitte Touche Tohmatsu, whose U.S. accounting arm is called Deloitte & Touche; Ernst & Young; KPMG; and PricewaterhouseCoopers. But Andersen wasn't the only major firm implicated in accounting scandals of the early 2000s. Deloitte & Touche, Ernst & Young, KPMG, and PwC have all faced legal heat in recent years thanks to accounting misdeeds.

In terms of how would-be accountants are being affected by the scandals, the accounting industry is refocusing on ethics. So if you interview for an accounting job, expect to be asked to shed light on your high ethical standards. There is also an increased focus on hiring accountants with real-world business experience in addition to formal accounting education, so be prepared to talk about the impact your experience will have on your job performance. And new and experienced accountants alike are being required to expand their knowledge base to include new accounting regulations—namely, 2002's Sarbanes-Oxley Act (or "Sarbox"), which did things like limit the amount of time senior accounting executives can spend working with a single audit client, create a new accounting industry oversight board called the Public Company Accounting Oversight Board, and introduce new regulations to which public companies (which comprise the bulk of the audit clients at big public accountancies) must adhere.

A note: Big Four public accounting firms—which focus on auditing clients' financial statements (thus verifying for investors that clients are being forthright about their financial health) but also include nonaudit lines of business such as actuarial work (risk analysis and management), tax consulting, human resources management, and merger and acquisition advice—are not the only career option for accountants. Many accountants work for midtier public accounting firms, such as Grant Thornton or Moss Adams, or for smaller firms; for government entities; or for corporations' in-house accounting or internal-audit departments. Many others go into business for themselves.

The Bottom Line

It's a good time to be looking for a job in public accounting firms. After contracting during the business slowdown of the early 2000s, hiring is now on the rise—especially, as demand for accounting services soar due to a newly healthy business climate, for experienced candidates who can come in and start contributing on day 1.

Far and away, the most positions available in public accounting are in audit, with tax coming in second. The need for forensic accountants—specialized accountants who focus on digging into clients' balance sheets to look for red flags—is growing as the industry and its clients look to rebuild their reputation. Demand for in-house corporate accounting and finance employees is expected to grow, as well.

Would-be accountants should exhibit analytical ability, leadership potential (if you advance in the Big Four and in many other firms, eventually you're going to be supervising teams of accountants), written and oral communication skills (since you're going to be communicating regularly with colleagues and clients), attention to detail (accounting is all about getting the details right), the ability to work independently as well as on teams (in most positions you'll be working with a team from your firm), a willingness to work long and hard when necessary (read: tax season), and high ethical standards.

What you'll get in return: a wealth of exposure to accounting issues, as well as a Big Four name on your resume—which can help you in a variety of business careers, if you ever decide to leave accounting.

How It Breaks Down

The Big Four

This group used to be the Big Five, but with the demise of Andersen in the wake of the Enron scandal, it's now the Big Four: Deloitte Touche Tohmatsu, Ernst & Young, KPMG, and PricewaterhouseCoopers. They are mammoth in size, with annual revenues in the tens of billions of dollars and tens of thousands of employees. These are the most prestigious employers for accounting grads. Why? Big Four clients are Fortune 1000 companies, which means that employees are exposed to complex accounting issues. A job with a Big Four firm is a great career move for someone entering the accounting profession. If, instead of moving up the ladder in your Big Four firm (to partner, preferably), you decide to work for another public accounting firm or to take an in-house position in industry or government—or even if you decide to hang out your own shingle—your Big Four experience will shine on your resume.

The central focus of the Big Four firms is audit services: the verification of the accuracy of clients' books. This also includes nonaudit lines of business, including actuarial work (risk analysis and management), tax consulting, human resources management, and merger and acquisition advice.

Other Public Accounting Firms

Although the Big Four get most of the publicity, there are many smaller, less well-known national players and regional public accounting firms that hire lots of people. Representative national firms include Grant Thornton, McGladrey

& Pullen, BDO Seidman, and Moss Adams. Within different regions of the country, there are also strong regional players that usually affiliate themselves with some national network of other such players. Insiders tell us that the hours are often a little better at these smaller firms than at the Big Four, the path to partner a little quicker, and the work itself more varied and interesting. If you go to a Big Four firm, your only responsibility for 3 months might be to audit the cash account at IBM. Ugh! According to one insider, at a regional firm you'll be a bigger fish in a smaller pond.

In-House Accounting

Whether publicly traded or not, every company has internal accountants to set budgets, manage assets, and track payroll, accounts payable and receivable, and other financial matters. For medium and large firms, the internal staff works closely with the public auditors at the fiscal year-end and with senior management and IT staff year round.

Controllers and CFOs at smaller firms often enjoy even more important and influential roles in running and developing the business. These jobs are just as demanding as those in public accounting.

Most accountants in the private sector stay in one place, in one job, working with the same colleagues, for extended periods. However, should you choose to move around, accounting skills are very portable.

Internal Audit Outsourcing

Some businesses prefer to outsource their internal audit functions to a third party. For these companies, and for auditors who want to work in this capacity, accounting firms like Jefferson Wells International are the answer.

Government

Although it's not the biggest blip on the radar of aspiring accountants, the government hires a lot of people with accounting skills. The biggest federal employers are traditionally the Department of Defense, the General Accounting Office, the Securities and Exchange Commission, and the Internal Revenue Service. In addition to monitoring individual and corporate tax returns, government accountants at the state and federal levels formulate and administer budgets, track costs, and analyze publicly funded programs.

Independent

As an accountant, you can always hang out your own shingle, individually or in partnership with other accountants, especially once you have your CPA. There is plenty of business preparing tax returns and advising small businesses, provided you have relevant expertise, such as a thorough knowledge of tax law. You will also need to market your services and manage your own business—time-consuming activities that not everyone enjoys.

Industry Trends

Sarbanes-Oxley and Its Results

In response to the corporate accounting scandals of the early 2000s, in 2002, the federal government introduced the Sarbanes-Oxley Act, which

- Created the Public Company Accounting Oversight Board (PCAOB), which can penalize accountancies and public corporations for accounting misdeeds.

- Requires more independent membership on corporate boards of directors.

- Forces public accounting firms to rotate audit partners off their current assignments once every 5 years.

- Requires public companies to create independent audit committees, which deal with their contracted accounting firm.

- Requires CEOs of public companies to sign off on the accuracy of their companies' financial statements.

These and other new rules and regulations in the Act create a more complex and expensive job for the public accounting firms auditing companies' books. In response, some smaller accounting firms have stopped auditing publicly traded clients, citing increased costs associated with such engagements. Accountancies that audit public companies (such as the Big Four), meanwhile, are in hog heaven. More complexity in corporate accounting regulations means more complex audit engagements, after all—and higher fees.

On the front lines in accounting, Sarbanes-Oxley has resulted in new work for accountants, because it requires companies to detail their financial reporting processes, and requires auditors to verify that those processes follow industry rules. As one insider puts it, "Sarbanes-Oxley calls for auditors to not only test and opine on the accuracy of the financial numbers a company releases, but to opine on the processes the company used to arrive at those numbers." About this work, the insider says, "You're not dealing with technical accounting issues; you're dealing with 'How did this invoice get paid?'"

More Scandalous Behavior

You break the rules, you pay a price. You'd think the Big Four public accounting firms would have gotten the idea by now. Apparently, though, they haven't—even after the demise of Arthur Andersen, which was essentially forced out of business by the government due to its role in the Enron accounting scandal; even after the fines and bad press all the Big Four firms have had to deal with over the past few years; even after all the talk coming from their mouths about a return to ethics, and the importance of rebuilding the public trust in accountants.

Even after, so far in 2004, the new PCAOB has denied one (small) public accounting firm the ability to audit public companies and has punished Ernst & Young for misdeeds by denying the firm the ability to take on new public audit clients for 6 months.

Even after all that, in 2004, the PCAOB, after limited inspections of the Big Four, declared that those firms' audits of public-company clients still had "significant" problems, meaning the wave of accounting scandals may not be fully over.

Trickle Down

The first ones to benefit from the downfall of Arthur Andersen were the rest of the Big Five (now the Big Four). Someone had to serve the accounting needs of Andersen's clients, largely major corporations—and the new Big Four were the obvious choice. The Big Four have seen strong revenue increases as a result starting in 2003. Now, in 2004, the second tier of public accounting firms, such as Crowe Chizek and Plante & Moran, are picking off more and more Big Four clients. This is happening in many cases because Big Four firms are ending audit relationships with companies they consider more risky to audit. Regardless, the second tier of accounting firms is about to enjoy a bigger bottom line as a result of the significant new clients coming their way. Meaning these are going to be good places to find jobs in coming months.

Changing Skills, Changing Job Titles

Accountants are becoming more integral to their employers' decision-making processes than ever. Rather than being simple bean counters, keeping track of companies' businesses without really having an impact on the direction of those businesses—even if they work in-house—accountants are enjoying a greater voice in strategic business decisions. Rather than just collecting data and presenting it to management, accountants are being called on to analyze the numbers and the business environment and then to tell management about how companies are truly performing, how they can be expected to perform moving forward, and what steps management might take to improve future performance. This new emphasis on strategic input in accounting means that it will be more important than ever for accountants to have a deep working knowledge of technology, leadership ability, an understanding of the broad business environment, and the ability to communicate with colleagues in a diversity of corporate departments and functions.

At the same time, new accounting specialties are emerging in response to a changing business world. The prevalence of the Internet means there's now a need for finance types with system-security and Internet strategy expertise. Globalization, and the cross-border transactions and international trade agreements that are so important to it, mean that the need for professionals with a specialization in international accounting is growing. Environmental regulations and the threat of related legal problems demand more environmental accountants. And increased regulatory scrutiny of the accounting industry and the business community as a whole, as well as the accounting industry's desire to rehabilitate its reputation by doing unassailable work, means that the field of forensic accounting—which involves seeking out corporate financial malfeasance and potential breaches in financial system security—is on the rise.

Industry Rankings

The Big Four

Big Four Public Accounting Firms, by 2003 Revenue			
Firm	Revenue ($M)	1-Year Change (%)	Employees
Deloitte Touche Tohmatsu	15,100	20.8	119,237
PricewaterhouseCoopers	14,683	6.4	122,820
KMPG International	12,160	13.4	100,000
Ernst & Young International	13,136	29.8	103,000
Sources: Hoover's; WetFeet analysis.			

Key Second-Tier Accounting Firms

A step down from the Big Four are a group of public accounting firms which are just a fraction of the size of Big Four firms in terms of revenue and number of employees, but are major league businesses compared to the majority of accounting firms. Some of these firms boast practice areas as diverse as the Big Four, while others are more specialized in focus. For instance, Moss Adams has a focus on West Coast businesses. In general, these companies' clients are smaller than those of the Big Four.

Second-Tier Public Accounting Firms, by 2003 Revenue

Firm	FYE	U.S. Net Revenue ($M)	1-Year Growth (%)	Employees
RSM McGladrey	4/03	580	1	4,400
Grant Thornton	12/02	400	5	3,127
BDO Seidman	6/02	353	−16	1,972
Crowe Group	3/03	247	12	1,400
BKD	5/03	216	2	1,500
Moss Adams	12/02	175	7	1,300
Plante & Moran	6/03	174	8	n/a
Clifton Gunderson	5/03	145	6	1,502
Virchow Krause & Co.	5/03	104	8	n/a
Larson, Allen, Weishair & Co.	10/02	84	6	n/a

Sources: Hoover's; *Public Accounting Report*'s "Top 100 for 2003"; WetFeet analysis.

Other Public Accounting Firms

Other Key Firms, by Region

Firm	Headquarters	Website
Northeast		
Amper, Politziner & Mattia	Edison, NJ	www.amper.com
Anchin, Block & Anchin	New York	www.anchin.com
Baker Newman & Noyes	Portland, ME	www.bnncpa.com
Beard Miller Co.	Reading, PA	www.beardmiller.com
Beers & Cutler	Washington, DC	www.beersandcutler.com
Berdon	New York	www.dberdon.com
Berry, Dunn, McNeil & Parker	Portland, ME	www.bdmp.com
Blum Shapiro & Co.	West Hartford, CT	www.bshapiro.com
Carlin, Charron & Rosen	Worcester, MA	www.ccrweb.com
Cherry Bekaert & Holland	Richmond, VA	www.cbh.com
Citrin Cooperman & Co.	New York	www.citrincooperman.com
J.H. Cohn	Roseland, NJ	www.jhcohn.com
Feeley & Driscoll	Boston	www.fdcpa.com
Freed Maxick & Battaglia	Buffalo, NY	www.freedmaxick.com
Friedman	New York	www.friedmanllp.com
Goldenberg Rosenthal	Jenkintown, PA	www.grgrp.com
Grassi & Co.	Lake Success, NY	www.grassicpas.com
Mahoney Cohen & Co.	New York	www.mahoneycohen.com
Marcum & Kliegman	Woodbury, NY	www.mkllp.com
Margolin, Winer & Evens	Woodbury, NY	www.mwellp.com
Marks Paneth & Shron	New York	www.markspaneth.com
Parente Randolph	Philadelphia, PA	www.parentenet.com
Reznick Fedder & Silverman	Bethesda, MD	www.rfs.com

Other Key Firms, by Region (cont'd)

Firm	Headquarters	Website
Rosen Seymour Shapss Martin & Co.	New York	www.rssmcpa.com
Rothstein, Kass & Co.	Roseland, NJ	www.rkco.com
Smart and Associates	Devon, PA	www.smartassociates.com
Stout, Causey & Horning	Hunt Valley, MD	www.scandh.com
Tofias	Cambridge, MA	www.tofias.com
Vitale, Caturano & Co.	Boston	www.vitale.com
Watkins, Meegan, Drury & Co.	Bethesda, MD	www.wmdco.com
Weiser	New York	www.mrweiser.com
Withum Smith & Brown	Princeton, NJ	www.withum.com

Southeast

Firm	Headquarters	Website
Berkowitz Dick Pollack & Brant	Miami	www.bdpb.com
Carr, Riggs & Ingram	Enterprise, AL	www.carrriggsingram.com
Decosimo	Chattanooga, TN	www.decosimo.com
Dixon Hughes	High Point, NC	www.dixon-hughes.com
Elliott Davis	Greenville, SC	www.edcocpa.com
Goodman & Co.	Norfolk, VA	www.goodmanco.com
Habif, Arogeti & Wynne	Atlanta	www.hawcpa.com
Horne CPA Group	Jackson, MS	www.hcpag.com
Kaufman Rossin & Co.	Miami	www.krco-cpa.com
Lattimore, Black, Morgan and Cain	Brentwood, TN	www.lbmc.com
Mauldin & Jenkins	Albany, GA	www.mjcpa.com
Morrison, Brown, Argiz & Farra	Miami	www.mba-cpa.com
Rachlin, Cohen & Holtz	Miami	www.rchcpa.com
Warren, Averett, Kimbrough & Marino	Birmingham, AL	www.wakm.com

Other Key Firms, by Region (cont'd)

Firm	Headquarters	Website
Midwest		
Alpern Rosenthal	Pittsburgh	www.alpern.com
Blackman Kallick Bartelstein	Chicago	www.bkbcpa.com
Blue & Co.	Indianapolis	www.blueandco.com
Clark, Schaefer, Hackett & Co.	Middletown, OH	www.cshco.com
Cohen & Co.	Cleveland	www.cohencpa.com
Doeren Mayhew	Troy, MI	www.doeren.com
Eide Bailly	Fargo, ND	www.eidebailly.com
Hill, Barth & King	Youngstown, OH	www.hbkcpa.com
Katz, Sapper & Miller	Indianapolis	www.ksmcpa.com
Kemper CPA Group	Vincennes, IN	www.kempercpa.com
Kennedy & Coe	Salina, KS	www.kcoe.com
Lurie Besikof Lapidus & Co.	Minneapolis	www.lblco.com
Olsen Thielen	St. Paul, MN	www.olsen-thielen.com
Rea & Associates	New Philadelphia, OH	www.reacpa.com
The Rehmann Group	Saginaw, MI	www.rehmann.com
Rubin, Brown, Gornstein & Co.	St. Louis	www.rbg.com
Schenck Business Solutions	Appleton, WI	www.schenckcpa.com
Schneider Downs & Co.	Pittsburgh	www.sdcpa.com
Sikich Group Worldwide	Aurora, IL	www.sikich.com
SS&G Financial Services	Cleveland	www.ssandg.com
Suby, Von Haden & Associates	Madison, WI	www.sva.com
Wipfli	Wausau, WI	www.wipfli.com
Yeo & Yeo	Saginaw, MI	www.yeoandyeo-cpa.com

Other Key Firms, by Region (cont'd)

Firm	Headquarters	Website
West		
Armanino McKenna	San Leandro, CA	www.amllp.com
Burr, Pilger & Mayer	San Francisco	www.bpmllp.com
Ehrhardt, Keefe, Steiner, & Hottman	Denver	www.eksh.com
Hein & Associates	Denver	www.heincpa.com
Holthouse Carlin & Van Trigt	Los Angeles	www.hcvt.com
Ireland San Filippo	San Jose, CA	www.isfllp.com
LeMaster & Daniels	Spokane, WA	www.lemasterdaniels.com
Miller, Kaplan, Arase & Co.	N. Hollywood, CA	www.millerkaplan.com
Mohler, Nixon & Williams	Campbell, CA	www.mohlernixon.com
Novogradac & Co.	San Francisco	www.novoco.com
Frank, Rimerman & Co.	Menlo Park, CA	www.fr-co.com
Singer Lewak Greenbaum & Goldstein	Los Angeles	www.slgg.com
Stonefield Josephson	Santa Monica, CA	www.sjaccounting.com
Weaver and Tidwell	Fort Worth, TX	www.weaverandtidwell.com

The Firms

- The Big Four

- Key Second-Tier Accounting Firms

The Big Four

These are the big daddies of accounting. They serve the biggest clients and offer the most job opportunities.

Deloitte & Touche LLP

1633 Broadway
New York, NY 10019
212-492-4000
www.us.deloitte.com

Overview

Deloitte & Touche, which traces its roots back to William Welch Deloitte, an Englishman, and George Touche, a Scotsman, is the U.S. accounting arm of Deloitte Touche Tohmatsu. The parent company, which employs more than 120,000 people in nearly 150 countries, recently separated its IT consulting arm, Deloitte Consulting, from the accounting arm—but, unlike the other members of the Big Four, it has not sold off its consulting business. (It had planned to spin Deloitte Consulting off into an entirely separate entity, to have been called Braxton, but called off the move due to poor market conditions. Deloitte Consulting works only for companies that are not audit clients of Deloitte & Touche.)

Deloitte focuses on providing audit services to midsized companies—those with less than $500 million in annual revenue. Like the other Big Four firms, it's experienced its share of PR difficulties in recent years. The firm has taken heat for its auditing work for Adelphia, whose accounting improprieties led to its bankruptcy and to securities fraud charges; recently, Adelphia sued Deloitte for failing to notify it that its founders were looting its coffers, as it alleges Deloitte should have. The firm has also been sued for $1 billion by the bankruptcy trustee for mortgage lender United Companies Financial Corp., who alleges that Deloitte colluded with the company's executives to pump up earnings figures.

Like other Big Four firms, Deloitte is beefing up staff in 2004 to handle additional business coming in as corporate America recovers from the early 2000s recession and to handle the additional work required as a result of Sarbanes-Oxley regulations. Hiring of people with knowledge of Sarbanes-Oxley, or with knowledge of process management or process engineering, has been especially strong.

Undergrads and grad students interested in careers at Deloitte should complete an online application, and check with their school to see whether Deloitte interviews on campus. If it does, they should go to Deloitte's campus presentations and sign up to interview on campus. If Deloitte doesn't go to your school, you can still apply online; if recruiters at the firm like what they see, they'll contact you to set up an initial phone interview.

The firm offers students internships in the spring (January to March) and summer (June to August), in areas of the firm including assurance, financial advisory services, enterprise risk services, human capital, solutions, and tax services.

The firm's website offers a helpful Where Do You Fit? tool (http://careers.deloitte.com/wdyf.aspx), designed to help visitors get an idea of where they might best fit within the firm.

Highlights

2004   As part of its staffing-up efforts, the firm is trying to lure back former employees with lucrative job offers. Deloitte is also offering referral bonuses to employees who connect the firm with "hot" candidates who end up working for the firm.

Indicted in a lawsuit brought by a pension fund over its role in the accounting scandal that has threatened to destroy European food company Parmalat.

2003   Makes *Working Mother* magazine's 2003 list of the "100 Best Companies for Working Mothers." (Like its Big Four brethren, Deloitte offers employees very good benefits.)

Pays $23 million to settle charges of faulty auditing of failed Kentucky Life Insurance, a client back in the 1980s.

2002   Deloitte Touche Tohmatsu's tax practice ranks first in Euromoney Legal Media Group's 2002 World's Leading Tax Adviser Survey, and its national practices also top the ranks in the United States, United Kingdom, Belgium, Hong Kong, and Japan.

Key Financial Statistics

2002 revenue: $5,930 million

1-year change: 1 percent

Note: 2002 was the most current revenue available at time of print.

Personnel Highlights

Number of employees, 2002: 28,203

1-year change: 3 percent

Ernst & Young International

5 Times Square
New York, NY 10036
212-773-3000
www.eyi.com

Overview

Ernst & Young (which traces its history back to Arthur Young & Co., founded in 1906, and Ernst & Ernst, founded in 1903) offers audit, internal audit, accounting advisory, online security, tax, and risk management services. The firm focuses on seven industry sectors: financial services; technology, communications, and entertainment; energy, chemicals, and utilities; industrial products; retail and consumer products; health sciences; and real estate, hospitality, and construction.

E&Y has been the most aggressive of the Big Four in terms of acquiring ex-Andersen clients. Like its Big Four counterparts, KPMG and Pricewaterhouse-Coopers, E&Y recently sold off its consulting arm to Capgemini in response to regulatory scrutiny of possible conflicts of interest implicit in auditing engagements for consulting clients.

Like the other members of the Big Four in the post-Enron/Arthur Andersen era, E&Y is facing heat for alleged misdeeds. Most recently, in July 2004, the SEC forbade the firm from taking on new audit clients for 6 months as a result of its relationship with PeopleSoft in the 1990s (in which E&Y acted as PeopleSoft's independent auditor despite developing and selling technology together). E&Y has also faced lawsuits, or the threat of same, over accounting misdeeds in audits of companies including HealthSouth, Tower Air, Cendant, and Time Warner. In addition, the firm is under scrutiny by the IRS for allegedly setting up extra-aggressive tax shelters for executives of client companies.

On the positive side of the scandal ledger, in 2004 a $2 billion lawsuit, brought against the firm by the FDIC and alleging that E&Y was guilty of fraud and negligence in its audit of a Chicago savings and loan in 2001, was thrown out of court.

In response to the scandals it's been embroiled in, the firm has done things like emphasize ethics training for employees, name a "quality czar," develop processes to double-check more audits in-house, disband the department offering high-net-worth individual tax services, become more selective in determining which of its clients it will continue to audit based on how risky those clients audits appear to the firm, and create a confidential ethics hotline.

If you're a student, check with your career center to see whether E&Y comes to your campus, and if so, how you can get an interview with the firm. If the firm doesn't come to your school, you can apply for jobs at the firm on its website.

Highlights

2004   Expected to hire about 2,500 undergrads, an increase of more than 20 percent from 2003.

Banned from taking on new audit clients for 6 months due to past conflicts of interest in its relationship with PeopleSoft.

A three-judge panel in Chicago rules that a $2 billion federal lawsuit against Ernst & Young in connection with the 2001 failure of Superior Bank, a Chicago savings and loan, is without merit.

Ranks 97th on *Fortune*'s list of the "100 Best Companies to Work For," the only Big Four firm to make the list this year.

2003   Accused of fraud for allegedly overcharging clients for travel expenses.

Settles illegal tax shelter charges with the IRS for $15 million.

CEO Rick Bobrow steps down after just a year on the job.

2002   With Rudy Giuliani, launches a new consulting and finance firm bearing the former NY mayor's name.

Key Financial Statistics

2003 revenue: $13,136 million

1-year change: 30 percent

Personnel Highlights

Number of employees: 103,000

1-year change: 18 percent

KPMG L.L.P.

345 Park Avenue
New York, NY 10154
212-758-9700
www.us.kpmg.com

Overview

KPMG LLP is the U.S. subsidiary of KPMG International. KPMG offers assurance, tax and legal, and financial advisory services. The "K" in the name refers
to Piet Klynveld, who founded Klynveld Kraayenhof & Co. in Amsterdam in
1917; the "P" refers to William Barclay Peat, who founded William Barclay Peat
& Co. in London in 1870; the "M" refers to James Marwick, who cofounded
Marwick, Mitchell & Co. in New York in 1897; and the "G" refers to Reinhard
Goerdeler, who was longtime chairman of Deutsche Treuhand-Gesellschaft
and later CEO of KPMG.

In the early 2000s KPMG spun off its IT consulting arm, selling 20 percent to
Cisco and bringing the rest public.

Like the other firms in the Big Four, KPMG has faced its share of legal and PR
headaches of late. In response to these and other accounting scandals, the firm
has taken actions including shaking up its tax business management, ending its
tax shelter business, increasing internal oversight of its businesses, and creating
a website where all the stakeholders in the changes in the accounting world
created by the Sarbanes-Oxley Act can visit and interact.

Like the other Big Four firms, KPMG has also benefited from the increase in
business that started gaining momentum in 2003, and the firm has ramped up
hiring as a result. If you're a student, check with your campus career center to
see whether KPMG comes to your campus; if you're not a student, or if you're

an experienced job candidate, you can apply online. KPMG offers internships, which typically lead to full-time jobs, in winter/spring and summer.

Highlights

2004   Shakes up management of tax business, letting several partners go.

2003   Accused of fraud, in the form of overbilling clients for travel expenses.

       SEC charges firm and four of its partners due to its failure to detect a $3 billion accounting fraud at Xerox.

2002   Censured by the SEC for auditing a money-market fund it was invested in.

Key Financial Statistics

2003 revenue: $4,630 million

1-yr. change: 35 percent

Parent company's 2003 revenue: $12,160 million

1-year change: 13 percent

Personnel Highlights

Number of employees: 18,000

1-yr. change: 2 percent

Parent company's number of employees: 100,000

1-year change: 2 percent

PricewaterhouseCoopers

1301 Avenue of the Americas
New York, NY 10019
646-471-4000
www.pwc.com

Overview

PricewaterhouseCoopers, the result of the 1998 merger of Price Waterhouse and Coopers & Lybrand, is the world's largest accounting firm. PwC has three main businesses: assurance and business advisory services (including financial and regulatory reporting), tax and legal services, and corporate finance and recovery. The firm sold its IT consulting arm to IBM in 2002. PwC makes more than half its revenue outside the United States, and has member firm offices in 768 cities in 139 countries.

Like the other members of the Big Four, PwC has had its share of recent legal and PR troubles. It is under the microscope currently due to its auditing work for the now-disgraced Tyco International and a high-profile gender discrimination lawsuit, and in recent years the firm has come under fire for overcharging clients for travel expenses and its role in client AMERCO's financial difficulties.

But, thanks to the extra work the firm is doing these days on audits and because of Sarbanes-Oxley, the firm is on a hiring binge, which looks to last at least into 2005. The news is especially good for experienced job candidates. Indeed, while PwC hired a record number of senior professionals in 2003, it looks to break that record in 2004, by nearly a third. All candidates should complete one of the firm's online career profiles, accessible at www.pwcglobal.com/ocp. Students should check with their school's career services offices to learn if and when PwC is coming to their campus. Experienced hires and students at schools where PwC does not recruit on campus can apply for jobs online.

Highlights

2004   Settles lawsuit alleging it overcharged clients for travel expenses for $54.5 million.

Sued by an employee for allegedly derailing her career via its corporate culture, which denies women access to the very opportunities that lead to partnership—things like informal networking events, golf outings, and other activities that result in greater access to clients and partners.

2003   AMERCO, a former client, sues PwC for $2.5 billion for its role in accounting misdeeds at the company.

Makes *Working Mother*'s 2003 list of the "100 Best Companies for Working Mothers."

SEC bars two PwC partners, who had overseen the audits of scandal-plagued MicroStrategy and Tyco International, from auditing public companies.

Is accused of fraudulently overbilling clients by hundreds of millions of dollars for travel-related expenses.

2002   IBM acquires PwC's consulting arm for $3.5 billion.

Key Financial Statistics

2003 revenue: $14,683 million

1-year change: 6 percent

Personnel Highlights

Number of employees: 122,820

1-year change: −1 percent

Key Second-Tier Accounting Firms

Some of these are national in focus, with offices and clients across the country. Others are more regional in focus. While they are not nearly as big as the Big Four, many of these firms offer robust training for young accountants, and they are a good alternative to the Big Four for some candidates.

BDO Seidman, LLP

130 East Randolph Street, Suite 2800
Chicago, IL 60601
312-240-1236
www.bdo.com

Overview

BDO Seidman is the seventh-largest accounting firm in the United States, coming in behind Grant Thornton near the top of the second tier of accounting firms. Its most important practice is its assurance practice, which audits client companies. The assurance practice includes a new risk consulting and advisory practice, which helps clients navigate the rapidly changing financial regulatory business risk environments. BDO Seidman also does business in tax and financial advisory, and it has a consulting practice, which helps clients choose and implement IT solutions. It also employs people in business development and financial advisory positions.

Other services offered via the firm's parent, BDO International, the fifth-largest accounting firm in the world, include human capital search (i.e., executive recruiting).

The firm focuses on midsized clients and operates out of some 35 locations. BDO also has alliances with independent accounting firms in 175 other offices, through a program called BDO Seidman Alliance. The parent company, which opened shop in 1963 and is headquartered in Belgium, has a total of some 600 offices in 100 companies around the world.

BDO Seidman is currently engaged in an ongoing dispute with the IRS over allegedly marketing abusive tax shelters. While the firm has done well in signing on new audit clients in recent times, it has been hard hit by decreasing demand for tax consulting services and by bad PR relating to its legal struggles. In response to weak returns to the bottom line, in late 2003 BDO Seidman replaced five of its governing board members and announced that the CEO was taking an indefinite leave of absence, and early in 2004 the firm pushed about 10 percent of its partnership out the door.

The firm is always on the lookout for talented experienced candidates, and it hires students into assurance associate, tax associate, and intern positions. Contact the office you want to work in for more information, as recruiting can differ from office to office.

Highlights

2004   Eliminates some 30 partners (around 10 percent) from its partnership ranks.

2003   Ordered by the IRS to turn over the names of clients that purchased certain tax shelters from the firm.

        Picks up 56 former Big Four clients.

Key Financial Statistics

2003 revenue: $350 million

Personnel Highlights

Number of employees: 1,972

BKD, LLP

Hammons Tower
901 East Saint Louis Street, Suite 1800
Springfield, MO 65801
417-831-7283
www.bkd.com

Overview

BKD, which does business in America's heartland states (with locations in
Arkansas, Colorado, Illinois, Indiana, Kansas, Kentucky, Missouri, Nebraska,
Ohio, Oklahoma, and Texas), traces its roots back to 1914 and the formation of
Clinton H. Montgomery & Co., the first public accountancy in Missouri. Today
the firm, ninth largest in the United States, is a member of Moores Rowland
International, an international association of independent accounting firms.

BKD offers assurance, tax, technology, financial planning, corporate finance,
and forensics and dispute services to individuals and companies in the following
industries: colleges and universities, construction, financial institutions, health care,
manufacturing and distribution, nonprofit and government, real estate, retail,
services, and transportation and utilities. BKD also offers accounting outsourc-
ing services, through which BKD performs internal-accounting functions such
as internal audits, financial statement preparations, payroll and sales tax return
preparation, controller and bookkeeping staffing, accounting systems design,
and accounting staff training to organizations lacking robust in-house accounting staff and procedures.

In response to the scandals that have rocked the accounting world, BKD has
created an independent advisory council to ensure it acts ethically.

BKD provides entry-level hires with some 100 hours of training in their first 18
months on the job. Entry-level hires are also matched with mentors within the

firm. Check with your school's career center to learn whether the firm comes to your campus, or apply online.

Highlights

2004   Joins forces with Bank Earnings Alliance, a management consultancy, to offer profit-improvement services to community banks and other financial services companies.

2003   Merger with EKW & Associates strengthens BKD's presence in Kentucky.

Ranked the third-best place to work in St. Louis.

2001   Olive LLP and Baird Kurtz & Dobson, each with a history dating back to the early 1900s, merge to form BKD.

Key Financial Statistics

2003 revenue: $216 million

1-year change: 2 percent

Personnel Highlights

Number of employees: 1,500

1-year change: 0 percent

Clifton Gunderson LLP

301 SW Adams Street, Suite 600
Peoria, IL 61602
309-671-4560
www.cliftoncpa.com

Overview

Clifton Gunderson is the 12th-largest accountancy in the United States. The firm offers assurance, tax, management and IT consulting, valuation, forensic, and other services to clients in industries including agribusiness, law, construction, auto dealership, financial services, health care, government, manufacturing, and nonprofit arenas.

The firm is growing its business via alliances with other businesses and mergers and acquisitions. Recent years have seen the firm merge with Wooden & Benson (2004); Network Technology Solutions (2003); Coughlin & Mann (2003); Zolondek, Strassels, Greene & Freed (2003); Effective Systems Consulting and Datahelp, Inc. (2002); Telesis Consulting (2002); Van Schooneveld & Co. (2001); and Fangmeyer and Fangmeyer CPAs (2001).

The firm's offices are largely autonomous, so cultural consistency doesn't necessarily exist across the firm (something that can be true even among the Big Four firms), but everyone at the firm has access to benefits that include flexible work arrangements, mentoring, training, tuition assistance, and professional certification assistance. The firm has offices in Arizona, California, Colorado, Illinois, Indiana, Iowa, Maryland, Missouri, New Mexico, Ohio, Texas, Virginia, Wisconsin, and the District of Columbia.

Experienced candidates should contact the office they're interested in and/or apply for jobs online; students can learn whether and when Clifton Gunderson is visiting their campus at

www.cliftoncpa.com/Careers/campuscalendar/calendar.asp.

Highlights

2004   Creates national valuation and forensic services practice.

2003   Merges with Wooden & Benson and Coughlin & Mann. Network Technology Solutions merges with Clifton Gunderson to form Clifton Gunderson Technology Solutions.

2002   Grows via mergers in locations including Arizona, Texas, the Mid-Atlantic states, Colorado, Wisconsin, and the Chicago area.

Key Financial Statistics

2003 revenue: $160 million

1-year change: 17 percent

Personnel Highlights

Number of employees: 1,502

1-year change: 7 percent

Crowe Chizek and Company LLC

330 East Jefferson Boulevard
South Bend, IN 46624
574-232-3992
www.crowechizek.com

Overview

A member of the Horwath International alliance of independent accounting firms, through which it does business outside the United States, Crowe Chizek offers assurance, tax, consulting, risk management, and technology services to clients in financial services, manufacturing, state and local government, education, auto dealership, wholesale and distribution, and other industries. The firm has offices in Florida, Illinois, Indiana, Kentucky, Michigan, Ohio, and Tennessee.

In existence since 1942, the firm is the eighth-largest accountancy in the United States. Crowe Chizek has been expanding via strategic acquisitions and investments.

The firm recruits on campus mainly at big Midwestern schools. To be considered for entry-level positions, you should send your resume to campus_recruiting @crowechizek.com. You can access a schedule of Crowe Chizek campus events in the careers section of the company's website. Experienced candidates should also visit the company's careers section to apply for jobs online.

Highlights

2004   Expands to East Coast with opening of New Jersey office.

Launches forensic services and investigations practice.

2003   Ranks number one among Central Midwest firms by *Accounting Today*.

Merges with Carrier & Co., strengthening its presence in Florida.

Merges with Kruse & Associates, strengthening its presence in Tennessee.

Is named top accounting firm at *Mergers & Acquisitions Advisor* magazine's "Academy Awards of Middle Market Mergers and Acquisitions."

2002 Opens a downtown Chicago office.

Acquires an interest in Castillo Miranda, a Mexican accounting and consulting firm.

Acquires R.V. Norene & Associates, a Chicago-area financial advisor.

Key Financial Statistics

2002 revenue: $165 million

Personnel Highlights

Number of employees, 2002: 1,400

Grant Thornton LLP

175 West Jackson Boulevard, 20th Floor
Chicago, IL 60604
312-856-0001
www.grantthornton.com

Overview

Grant Thornton, which is typically at or near the top of the second tier of U.S. public accounting firms, provides clients with assurance and advisory, tax, valuation, compensation and benefits, mergers and acquisitions advisory, and management advisory services. The firm serves clients in nonprofit, real estate, hospitality, government and government contracting, construction, consumer and industrial products, financial services, and technology industries. It has offices in 29 states throughout the United States, including the District of Columbia.

The firm did well in the sweepstakes to take on former Arthur Andersen offices clients after that firm failed. It is also taking on former Big Four clients as those firms become more selective about what companies they want to retain as clients. Indeed, Grant Thornton has been doing very well of late, with the greatest 2003 revenue growth among public accounting firms.

Grant Thornton recruits at many campuses. Check with your career services office to learn if and when the firm is coming to your campus. If the firm doesn't recruit at your campus, or if you're an experienced candidate, you should contact the office where you want to work (for contact details, visit www.grantthornton.com/contact/locations.asp) or search for open positions on the firm's website.

Grant Thornton clearly wants to play with the big boys. And, like the big boys, Grant Thornton faced scandals of its own: In 2002, it was found guilty of negligence in its relationship with client Carnegie International.

Highlights

2004   Places 19th in the league tables for mergers and acquisitions advisory, meaning it's a significant player in the world of M&A deal-making.

Creates National Tax Quality Assurance position as part of effort to strengthen internal oversight.

Ranks first in revenue growth among accounting firms in the 2003 rankings in the *Public Accounting Report's Annual Survey of National Firms.*

2002   Is found guilty of negligence in relationship with client Carnegie International.

Key Financial Statistics

2003 revenue: $459 million

1-year change: 15 percent

Personnel Highlights

Number of employees: 3,127

1-year change: 8 percent

The Firms

Larson, Allen, Weishair & Co., LLP

220 South Sixth Street, Suite 300
Minneapolis, MN 55402
612-376-4500
www.larsonallen.com

Overview

Founded in 1953, LarsonAllen offers assurance, executive search, information security, litigation and valuation, and tax services to clients in the auto dealership, construction, technology, financial services, health care, manufacturing and distribution, nonprofit, government, and education industries. Like other second-tier accounting firms in the United States, the firm is expanding via mergers with smaller firms.

LarsonAllen, which is the 14th-largest accounting firm in the United States, has offices in various locations in Minnesota, as well as in St. Louis, Philadelphia, and Charlotte, North Carolina. The firm is affiliated with the Baker Tilly International network of independent accounting and consulting firms.

LarsonAllen recruits on campus at schools including the University of Minnesota—Duluth, the University of Minnesota's Carlson School of Management, Saint John University, University of Wisconsin—La Crosse, the University of St. Thomas, the University of Northern Iowa, North Carolina State, Carlson School of Management, University of North Carolina—Chapel Hill, St. Cloud State University, Minnesota State University—Mankato, and North Dakota State University.

Highlights

2004   Joyce Miller and Associates, a Philadelphia accountancy, joins LarsonAllen.

2003   Beibl Ranweiler, a Minnesota accountancy, joins LarsonAllen.

       Stienessen, Schlegel & Co., a Minnesota accountancy, joins LarsonAllen.

       Expands auto dealership, manufacturing and distribution, health care, and government audit practices.

2002   Grows Minnesota presence with a series of mergers with smaller firms.

Key Financial Statistics

Not available.

Personnel Highlights

Number of employees: about 650

McGladrey & Pullen, LLP

3600 American Boulevard West, 3rd Floor
Bloomington, MN 55431
952-835-9930
www.mcgladrey.com

Overview

Founded in 1926, McGladrey & Pullen provides accounting and audit services primarily to owner-managed middle-market clients in industries including financial services, government and nonprofit, health care, manufacturing and distribution, hospitality, and construction. McGladrey & Pullen is an independent member of RSM International, the sixth-largest worldwide accounting and consulting organization. McGladrey & Pullen is allied with RSM McGladrey, a consulting firm owned by H&R Block, and together they offer clients an array of business-advice services.

The firm offers, in many of its locations, internships during the busy season in tax or auditing, and in some instances, a combination of the two. Depending on specific office needs, there are occasional opportunities for summer internships.

Scholarships are available from the firm at a variety of colleges and universities in the United States, typically through the schools' departments of accounting. Ask your accounting department to see whether this program is available on your campus.

The firm offers some students a fast-track accounting program, in which McGladrey pays for schooling in return for a 3-year work commitment.

Highlights

2004   Special relationship with the University of St. Thomas's new MS in Accountancy program guarantees students internships.

2003   The Center for Ethical Business Cultures and Minnesota Society of Financial Service Providers name McGladrey & Pullen a finalist in their 2003 Minnesota Business Ethics Awards program.

Key Financial Statistics

RSM McGladrey 2003 revenue: $416 million

Personnel Highlights

Number of employees: 4,400

The Firms

Moss Adams LLP

1001 Fourth Avenue, 31st Floor
Seattle, WA 98154
206-223-1820
www.mossadams.com

Overview

Tracing its history back to 1913, when it was founded following the enactment of the first U.S. income tax, Moss Adams offers accounting, tax, and consulting services to middle-market clients in a variety of industries. The firm, which has some 180 partners, is a member of the Moores Rowland International group of independent accountancies. Moss Adams's three affiliate companies allow it to offer clients services in areas like investment banking, royalty compliance, and asset management, and Moss Adams Advisory Services offers consulting services in areas like claims resolution, information technology, litigation, mergers and acquisitions, risk management, corporate finance, and valuation. The firm has offices in Washington, Oregon, California, and New York.

The firm is currently in hiring mode, especially for its several new offices in Southern California.

Students and experienced candidates alike who are interested in Moss Adams should start the process by completing the firm's online application. Students should then submit a resume, cover letter, and transcript at their school's careers office. Moss Adams will then notify those students whom it wants to meet on campus. Students who want to work in a specific office should note that fact on their application materials and in their interviews.

Highlights

2004   Creates position of Independent Ethics Advisor to enhance internal oversight.

2003   Names new CEO and COO.

2002   Named the Firm of the Year by the Washington Society of Certified Public Accountants.

Key Financial Statistics

2003 revenue: $180 million

1-year change: 13 percent

Personnel Highlights

Number of employees: 1,300

Plante & Moran, LLP

27400 Northwestern Highway
Southfield, MI 48034
248-352-2500
www.plante-moran.com

Overview

Founded in 1924, Plante & Moran offers assurance, tax, personal financial advisory, litigation and valuation, consulting, technology consulting, and corporate finance services. Its clients include companies and organizations in the construction and real estate, auto dealership, financial services, health and human services, manufacturing and distribution, nonprofit and public sector, and professional services industries. The firm claims that it strives to combine the efficiencies and professionalism of larger firms with a small-firm culture and attention to client service. Plante & Moran is an affiliate of Moores Rowland International, a network of independent accountancies.

Plante & Moran has offices at a variety of locations in Michigan and Ohio, and recruits at the following schools: Albion, Aquinas, Baldwin-Wallace, Bowling Green State University, Calvin, Central Michigan University, Eastern Michigan University, Ferris State, Grand Valley State University, Heidelberg, Hillsdale, Hope, John Carroll, Miami Ohio, Michigan State University, Northwood University, Oakland University, Ohio State, Ohio University, University of Findlay, University of Michigan, University of Michigan Dearborn, University of South Carolina, University of Toledo, Walsh, Wayne State University, and Western Michigan University.

The firm offers internships in the winter/spring and summer to accounting, finance, and management information systems students. For more information on internship opportunities, contact your campus career center or visit the firm's website.

The firm is currently ramping up staffing. But be prepared to take a personality test if you apply for a job here; the firm not only uses the tests in its experienced-hire recruiting, but sells them to clients as well.

Nineteen percent of the firm's partners are female—the highest percentage among big accounting firms in the United States. Great benefits are part of the reason for this; employees here get benefits like sabbaticals, small breakfast meetings bringing together partners and employees, and other female- and employee-friendly programs.

Highlights

2004   Makes *Fortune*'s 2004 list of the "100 Best Companies to Work For"—its sixth straight year on the list.

Expands into the Chicago area with acquisition of Gleeson, Sklar, Sawyers & Cumpata; the merger makes Plante & Moran the tenth-largest accounting firm in the United States.

2002   Named Southfield Business of the Year by the Southfield Chamber of Commerce.

Key Financial Statistics

2003 revenue (including Gleeson, Sklar, Sawyers & Cumpata): $191 million

Personnel Highlights

Number of employees (including Gleeson, Sklar, Sawyers & Cumpata): 1,300

Virchow, Krause & Company, LLP

10 Terrace Court
Madison, WI 53718
800-362-7301
www.virchowkrause.com

Overview

Virchow Krause, which has some 125 partners and about 350 total CPAs, provides tax, accounting, audit, information technology, Internet strategy, human resources, financial staffing, business valuation, dispute resolution, employee benefits, risk management, insurance brokerage, wealth management, payroll and bookkeeping, and mergers and acquisitions services to middle market clients. Clients come from industries including education, construction and real estate, financial services, auto dealership, health care, manufacturing and distribution, nonprofit, and the public sector.

The firm grew drastically in 1999 through its merger with Schumaker Romanesko Associates. In 2003 it was the 13th-largest accountancy in the United States. It now has some 13 offices in Michigan, Minnesota, Wisconsin, and Illinois.

Virchow Krause recruits at Carthage College, Luther College, Marquette University, St. Benedict's, St. Cloud State University, St. John's, St. Thomas University, the University of Minnesota, and the University of Wisconsin at Eau Claire, Green Bay, La Crosse, Madison, Milwaukee, Oshkosh, Platteville, and Whitewater. Experienced hires can apply for jobs on the firm's online career center.

The firm is an independent member of Baker Tilly International, a global network of accountancies.

Highlights

2004   Expands into Chicago market with acquisition of KGN Financial Group.

Merges with Global Business Strategies, a Wisconsin global business services company. Global Business Strategies will help the firm better serve middle market clients looking to expand internationally.

2003   Merges with Detroit-based firm Nemes Allen.

Key Financial Statistics

2003 revenue: $104 million

1-year change: 11 percent

Personnel Highlights

Not available.

On the Job

- Public Accounting Roles

- Corporate Accounting Roles

- Real People Profiles

Accounting concerns itself with the day-to-day operations of bookkeeping. Accountants balance the books, track expenses and revenue, execute payroll, and pay the bills. They also compile all of the financial data needed to issue a company's financial statements in accordance with government regulations.

Accountants are taking a step away from the ledger sheets and are becoming essential to every successful business team. They're the ones who understand the language of money and a company's complex financial situation. Consequently, accountants are increasingly being called on to offer advice and even make business decisions based on hard facts rather than on speculation or gut instinct.

To be sure, an accountant's day-to-day work is still very different from that of a lion tamer, especially for those who are just entering the field. Most public accountants, for example, still need to know the specifics of tax law and must file audits that meet the Generally Accepted Accounting Principles (GAAP). Here, there's little room for people who want to think outside of the box. The box has been well thought out, and it's the accountant's job to make sure a company's records fit inside it and are in lockstep with the law.

There are many jobs for accountants in accounting firms; in in-house accounting departments for corporations; and in local, state, and federal government entities. Far and away, the most positions available in public accounting are in audit, with tax being the next most important area of focus.

Public Accounting Roles

By law, every business has to file paperwork with the government. The IRS, for example, requires year-end tax statements. Public accountants create and file such reports. While you can work at a public accounting firm without a license, in any given project, someone on a team of accountants must have a license and sign off on the final documents. Public accountants can have many responsibilities, but the field generally breaks down into two main functions: preparing a company's year-end tax statements and external auditing.

Public accountants can work at firms of varying size, from independent shops to the Big Four. The Big Four are mammoth in size; each has annual revenues in the tens of billions of dollars. These are the most prestigious employers because Big Four clients are Fortune 1000 companies. Either you'll move up the ladder, or, if you decide to go to work for another public accounting firm, an in-house accounting position in industry, or the government—or decide to hang out your own shingle—your Big Four experience will shine on your resume.

If you want to set up your own shop, having a CPA license is a requirement. Consequently, most practitioners working in public accounting are licensed CPAs. If they're not, they are working towards taking the exam or thinking about entering private accounting—or getting out altogether.

Big Four firms' central focus is external audit services: the verification of the accuracy of clients' books. External auditing involves examining a company's financial statements and reporting procedures to make sure the information is accurate. By law, an external auditor must work for a firm outside the company that's being audited to ensure objectivity and adequate protection against fraud. Consequently, external auditors must have a much greater understanding of the law and the Generally Accepted Accounting Principles than internal auditors.

On the Job

Staff Audit Accountant

Ask a few auditors what they do, and the answers will be pretty similar. Most audit work involves poring over the client's books, conducting tests on the income and expense statements, and telling the general public that there's been no material misstatement. At the most junior levels, accountants will be assigned less-complex areas of the balance sheet, such as fixed assets and cash, where there's less risk of confusion and error. At the senior level and above comes responsibility for managing several accountants on a project as well as maintaining contact with the client's accounting department.

The job involves lots of writing, from documenting different accounting systems or describing the procedures involved in testing a client's control structure to writing memos to the client requesting information. All staff-level work is reviewed on a day-to-day basis by a senior or manager. According to insiders, much of your first year as an audit accountant is about getting acclimated to the work environment and to working with clients. In the second year, you'll learn more of the skills necessary to supervise engagements at the senior level.

Assistants and staff auditors spend the bulk of their time at the client site, working on one project at a time. Some Big Four firms have even instituted "hoteling," a system under which most auditors don't get their own office until they reach a senior manager rank. An audit can last from a week to a year, and is usually staffed by at least one assistant or staff member, one senior, and one manager.

A Day in the Life of a Staff Audit Accountant

7:30   Get up, get dressed. Khakis and a polo shirt on this engagement. (Glad we have a client with a business-casual policy!)

8:20   Pull into parking lot at the client site.

8:45   Check voice mail and e-mail; skim the newspaper.

9:00   Pick up client's accounts receivable paperwork. Ask client to pull cash receipts, invoices, and bills of lading. Looks like there's plenty to check out here.

9:30   Continue to log accounts receivable.

10:30   Client's accounting clerk brings in check copies and invoices. Looks like a 4-hour job. Have a quick chat with manager over cubicle partition. She wants to have the AR done by tomorrow at lunchtime.

11:45   Lunch. Pile into cars and head over to a nearby Chinese place with the rest of the audit team.

12:45   Back at work. Keep going on those accounts receivable.

3:00   Identify three problem invoices out of 50. Discuss with senior accountant and with client's accounts receivable clerk, who explains two of the problems.

3:45   Write up third problem as an exception; propose adjustment to client's balance sheet. That went pretty smoothly.

4:00   Start looking at accounts receivable for collectibility. Check out client's aged AR report for $5 million; pick out some big ones due over 90 days. Talk to client's AR manager about the outstanding amounts to gauge the likelihood that the firm will be able to collect on those outstanding invoices.

5:30   It's a coworker's birthday today, so the team is going out to dinner. Mmm.

Senior Audit Accountant

The major difference between the staff and senior level is that at the senior level you are reviewing other people's work as well as doing your own. Seniors are also generally assigned to more than one client. You will be required to specialize in an industry. One insider tells us, "It can be difficult scheduling your time and managing your staff." But almost all senior-level insiders agree that the increased responsibility and autonomy are a welcome change from the drudgery of staff-level work.

A Day in the Life of a Senior Audit Accountant

8:30   Arrive at the office; check voice mail and e-mail. Eat a quick bagel at my desk while reading the *New York Times* online.

9:00   Spend some time preparing audit instruction packets. I'm currently supervising an audit of the pension plan on a company that has a large number of subsidiaries. As supervisor, I'm responsible for putting together and sending out packets to other audit teams around the country, instructing them on how to audit the individual subsidiaries of the client. This involves writing a memo detailing all of the steps involved in the audit and preparing the packets. In the packet, I include an audit program, the company's most recent work papers, and packages from actuaries. E-mail packet to all on the recipient list.

10:30   Start working on the audit of the client's overall pension plan. This involves looking at the company's investments and the contributions it made to the pension plan, as well as the year-end expenses that it still owes. I also make sure all of the proper controls were in place and ensure that the benefit payments adhere to the company's pension plan document. I come across a detail in the plan I haven't seen before, and I direct my question about it via voice mail to the appropriate client contact.

12:30   Grab a quick lunch at the burrito place around the corner.

1:15   Put together financial statements for the subsidiaries of the client. Basically this involves showing what receivables they have and what benefits they paid out, and describing the pension plan. Make a quick run to Central Files to get the client's work papers from last year.

3:00 Check voice mail. There's an urgent message from another client, which has a 10-Q that needs to be done right away. Drop what I'm doing and get to work on this report. Make sure the numbers in the report properly reflect the numbers that I audited. Check to make sure that every number in the 10-Q is accounted for—that is, it has some form of detail behind it showing what the number consists of—and check the amounts for reasonableness based on this detail. The public (investors) reads the 10-Q, so I've got to be 100 percent sure of its accuracy.

4:00 Take a break to hang out with a couple of guys on the audit team. Discuss whether Scottie Pippen belongs on the NBA's 50 Greatest Players list; decide he doesn't.

4:15 Back at desk, compile all the queries I have for the client from today.

6:00 Head home. Busy season is over; no more burning the midnight oil.

On the Job

Staff Tax Accountant

At the junior levels, tax accounting involves tax compliance, or the research and preparation of tax returns. Tax work is generally structured: Supervising senior accountants check out the work of staff and assistant accountants, managers recheck it, and senior managers or partners sign off on the returns.

Tax consulting, which is usually the responsibility of those at more senior levels, involves researching tax issues and advising corporations, trusts, and partnerships on the tax implications of various actions.

Unlike auditors, tax staff members get to spend most of their time in the home office. While January to April is the primary busy season, corporations and partnerships often extend tax-filing deadlines, which means that tax staff accountants have secondary busy seasons in the summer and fall.

A Day in the Life of a Staff Tax Accountant

7:30   Get up; have a bowl of cereal. Got to buy more bananas this weekend.

8:30   Arrive at the office, check e-mail. Looks like the daily tax report is in.

8:40   Message from senior manager, who has some new projects to dive into as soon as my current batch of returns is finished. Busy season is heating up!

8:50   Load my tax-preparation application and start working on a return. This one is pretty straightforward.

12:00   Lunch. Head out for a sandwich with the team.

1:00   Back at work. Looks like this return will be done right on schedule.

1:30   Uh-oh. The client didn't provide a complete listing of asset additions for the year, so the depreciation can't be calculated. Call manager, who gets in touch with the client. Start on a new return while waiting for the data.

3:30   Manager drops off a fax from the client. Run depreciation program. Finish up return and print it out.

4:00   Hand completed return to manager, then move on to the next one.

6:00   Order pizza with team. If this weren't busy season, we'd be home by now.

8:00   Finish second return; decide to print it out in the morning. Time to call it a day.

Other Public Accounting Jobs

Senior Accountant

This is the second level in the public accounting hierarchy. After a year or two at a public accounting firm, your paycheck improves and you might get sent out alone to run an audit. Depending on your firm, you might begin supervising teams of other accounts, so now is the time to take your CPA. In the states that have such prerequisites, you'll have logged enough hours by this point. This is also when a lot of accountants—as many as eight out of ten—leave their firms for some form of private corporate accounting.

Manager

This is a watershed position at a public accounting firm. If you get to this point, the firm thinks you're partner material, and you're probably giving the idea serious thought. You don't do as much hands-on auditing anymore, although managers often handle sensitive issues such as an important client's creative bookkeeping. Mainly, you plan and assemble audit teams and allocate their time at various jobs. At the end of an audit, you report back to a partner, who signs off on your work. This is a 5- to 7-year test with significant competition from your peers who are also on the partner track.

Partner

You made it! It probably took you 10 or more years to work your way through. Now you sign off on audits, work on client development (that is, bringing in the business), and train younger accountants. Oh, and you also collect a salary in the six-figure range.

Corporate Accounting Roles

When most people think of accounting, they imagine a public accountant who has passed an exam to become a state-licensed certified public accountant, or CPA. But companies large and small generally have their own staff accountants to advise management and to perform internal audits and day-to-day bookkeeping. In addition to the private sector, city, county, state, and federal bureaucracies also employ a large number of accountants.

Internal Auditor

Big, complex companies and companies operating in complex regulatory environments often employ internal auditors, whose role is to make sure that the company's financial records are in order and that operations are not being affected by mismanagement or fraud. Usually, they spend a lot of time analyzing the company's operational processes, information systems, financial systems, and controlling systems to confirm that the company is operating efficiently and is not being harmed (or in danger of being harmed), legally or financially, by malfeasance. Specializations within this job function include electronic data processing auditor, environmental auditor (who ensures that the company is not running afoul of environmental regulations), engineering auditor, bank auditor, and health care auditor.

Management Accountant

Management accountants, also known as corporate or private accountants, are in-house accountants. They track the finances of the companies they work for, overseeing profit-and-loss statements and balance sheets for everything from individual departments or product lines to the company as a whole. Management accountants may be responsible for planning and overseeing budgets and adjusting budgets periodically based on overall business strategy and the performance of various areas of the company given the budgets on which they're working. Other responsibilities may include forecasting financial performance; overseeing and reducing costs, for instance, by recommending and overseeing the implementation of new sales force–management software for the sales department of their company; or managing the investments of their company, with possible aims of increasing return on investment, increasing cash flow, or minimizing investment risk, depending on the strategic needs of the company.

Management accountants may also be responsible for preparing reports for outside parties and regulatory authorities—for instance, preparing tax returns, annual reports for investors, lender-required reports on the financial health of the company, or filings with the Securities and Exchange Commission. The precise details of the management accountant's job description can vary tremendously from company to company and industry to industry, but in every case they will need to possess or develop an intimate understanding of their company's business and the business and regulatory environment in which it operates.

Following are a few sample management accounting jobs.

Budget and Credit Analysts

The budget side plans and manages corporate finances over a 12-month or longer period. They present findings and recommendations either themselves or through a controller. The government also employs thousands of budget analysts to do the same type of work for public programs and expenditures. Credit specialists focus on whether customers or institutional clients can repay a loan or credit line. Banks are the biggest employers for these analysts.

Controller

Controller is a catchall title for a key financial officer at a corporate firm. The responsibilities and pay will vary considerably depending on the size of the firm. Controllers generally leave most of the actual number juggling to junior accountants and take a more strategic role in the support side of the business, planning the allocation of various funds throughout the company.

Real People Profiles

Staff Accountant

Age: 23

Years in business: 1.5

Education: BS, accounting

Hours per week: 40 in the off-season; 65 during tax season (mid-February to mid-April)

Size of company: 75 employees

Certification: working toward CPA

Annual salary: $40,000 including bonuses

What do you do?

I prepare tax returns for individuals, corporations, pension plans, and estates. Our firm is split into four departments: the audit department, which does attest work; the bookkeeping department; the information technology consulting department; and the tax department, where I work. We do compliance work and tax returns and we deal with other tax-related issues, such as letters from the IRS.

What did you do before?

I was in college. This is my first job after I got out of school.

How did you get your job?

I moved to Albuquerque, and I had no idea where I would work. I found this firm through the newspaper, but I also searched for jobs on the Internet. I sent out a lot of resumes.

What are your career aspirations?

I want to pass the CPA exam. I'm halfway there now. I haven't really decided on a long-term plan. I've played around with going to law school. Right now, I think I'd like to specialize in estate planning, but I haven't decided if it will be from the CPA angle or from the legal angle.

What kinds of people do well in this business?

People who are friendly and personable do well. It's important to have a good personality. You also have to be intellectually capable of picking up things relatively quickly. They don't expect you to do things flawlessly at first, but things do need to be done well and mostly correct in a reasonable amount of time.

We have ten partners and umpteen managers with very diverse personalities, and I answer to every one of them. You have to be able to interact with different individuals, so you have to learn for whom you do what and with whom you can and can't joke.

This isn't as true at my level, but when you go up a level or two, you really have to be a salesperson. They expect you to bring in clients, so you have to go to meetings and functions and really be out there in the business world to show that you're doing things to generate business.

What do you really like about your job?

I like the flexibility. We work really hard 3 months of the year, but the rest of the year is flexible. I don't know if that's true in the accounting business in general or just at this firm. If I need time off, I can take it; I can work from 9 to 5 or from 8 to 4 or from 7 to 3 if I want to.

What do you dislike?

I don't like the busy season. There are points when you'll have 3 or 4 weeks' worth of work on your desk, and you just say, "Oh, goodness, what do I do next?" I work from 7 a.m. to 7 p.m. during the tax season, Monday through Friday, and then 1 weekend day, too.

What is the biggest misconception about this job?

There's still that bean-counter stereotype. There are some of those people around, but they are humans underneath.

Looking back on your career or job search, what do you wish you had done differently?

I didn't know I was moving to Albuquerque until a month before the move. I went to school in Fargo, North Dakota, and I went through the recruiting process and had accepted a job with one of the Big Four in Minneapolis. I was bummed when I found out my husband and I had to move to Albuquerque. There are only two big firms here, and when I didn't get a job at one of them I thought, "Oh, I'll have to work at some rinky-dink firm." It turned out to be for the best. I talk to my friends who are in the big firms, and there's a lot more stress there.

How can someone get a job like yours?

It's pretty easy to get an accounting job if you're in college. Go through the recruiting process in the fall. Visit accounting-jobs websites and read the classifieds in newspapers. There are a lot of different opportunities.

Tax Accountant

Age: 24

Years in business: 2.5

Education: BS, accounting

Hours per week: 60 to 70 hours, with a 30-minute lunch, during tax season; 40 to 50, with a 1-hour lunch, otherwise

Size of company: 50 employees

Certification: none

Annual salary: $41,500

What do you do?

Tax compliance and consulting. We work with midsize and small businesses, and individuals. We primarily service middle-market clients. I work on tax returns, develop tax-saving strategies, and help clients plan their taxes for the following year. I do a lot of compliance work—preparing tax returns and various other forms. Tax planning involves a lot of research. We often have to research various tax databases for the proper treatment of issues that may arise.

How did you get your job?

I got my first job through my college placement office. I had just over 2 years of experience when I decided to move to Phoenix. I looked up headhunters in the phone book, called a couple, came out, and met with them. One set up interviews, for which I came back, and I picked a company. I knew I wanted to stay in public accounting and do tax work. It's easy to find financial headhunters in the yellow pages.

What are your career aspirations?

I'd like to be controller of a multi-entity, family-owned and -managed company (basically a family-run company with several types of businesses). I like family-owned companies because of the more personal ownership complexities that arise; the owners have their heart and soul in the business—they have a very personal connection to it. Multi-entity provides a more complex company structure that will keep the work interesting. To get there, I'll continue in public accounting a little longer, after which I'll switch to an internal position in the private sector. For now, public accounting is a good place to be for exposure and experience.

What kinds of people do well in this business?

Hard workers who are very detail-oriented. You have to juggle several tasks at one time and be very organized. You also need to be a good people person when you get to the In-Charge level.

What do you really like about your job?

It's challenging. I get to figure stuff out. I do learn a lot, which I really enjoy. Different things come up on every return. By seeing what another accountant did last year, I learn new ways of handling a particular tax problem. I also pick up tips from the In-Charge's suggestions. On the whole, it's a great way to learn the profession.

What do you dislike?

Sometimes it's very monotonous. I have almost no contact with people outside of the office, including clients. I was surprised about the lack of client contact— but this is specific to tax people. There are also long hours during the busy season. Worst of all, the CPA exam. (I probably need say no more.)

What is the biggest misconception about this job?

That accountants get a lot of time off in the summer. We still do tax returns and consulting during the summer. That's when we handle returns that got extensions. We also file any amended returns and respond to notices from the

IRS. If the IRS comes back to us, then we have to refile a new return, which almost always takes place in the summer.

Looking back on your career or job search, what do you wish you had done differently?

Spent more time looking into the various opportunities available. I wish I'd found out more about corporate accounting and other kinds of accounting. Coming out of college, the first thing that comes around is what you want. I knew I wanted to do tax rather than auditing where you have to travel a lot and certainly not always to exciting places.

Although I do love to travel, auditors work a lot while they are on the road so they can wrap everything up that they need to while they are at the client. But I might have looked into opportunities working for an internal tax department. It's also important to take the time to make sure the next move is right when you leave a company. It's no secret that many people do public accounting for a couple of years, get their license, and then move on. But you have to like your firm during that time.

How can someone get a job like yours?

Contact the HR person at any public accounting firm, or a headhunter, and use your college placement offices. It's not hard as long as you have the right course work in school. With a degree in accounting, you should be able to get a job. You don't even need tax-specific accounting classes, it just helps in interviews.

On the Job

Senior Tax Consultant

Age: 36

Years in business: 10

Education: BS, accounting and finance; Master's in tax accounting

Hours per week: 40; 60 during peak season

Size of company: 6 employees

Certification: CPA

Annual salary: $80,000

What do you do?

I work as a tax consultant for a small accounting firm. We serve businesses—usually small business—and high-net-worth individuals. We prepare tax returns and help clients figure out their financial and tax strategies, of course, but because it's such a small firm, there's a wide variety of work beyond that for me to do. For instance, since we conduct tax seminars, some days I have to answer questions that seminar participants have. Or I might have to consult with a client's lawyer in a divorce case.

How did you get your job?

I started my career by interning at one of what was then the Big Eight. After that, I took a staff job at Arthur Andersen and proceeded on a general accounting track. After 3 years, I specialized in in-patriate and expatriate tax. Then I took a little career detour and tried to start a career in fashion design, while working part-time as an in-house accountant for a clothing company. That didn't work out, so I took a job as an editor at a magazine. Neither of those jobs could pay for the kind of life I want to live, so I eventually turned back to accounting. I got my current job via an online job board, and I like it because it's a small firm, and I can do general accounting again.

What are your career aspirations?

I'd like to keep branching into other areas, such as tax education and tax seminars. And manual writing—I like writing.

What kinds of people do well in this business?

You've got to be detailed and analytical. You've got to be able to self-review. You're always dealing with people, on the phone or in person, so you've got to have good people skills. Taxes can make people emotional, so you've got to be able to calm clients while explaining tax technicalities to them in clear, understandable language. And you have to do a lot of e-mailing, so writing skills are just as important as people skills.

What do you really like about your job?

I like that I get to deal with a variety of clients, from rich individuals to start-up mom-and-pop businesses. I like the international element of the in-patriate or expatriate tax work I do; I have to understand people and rules from a variety of places. I get satisfaction out of doing tax research—finding cases and rulings that I can use to help my clients. And one thing I like about being at a senior level is interacting with and reviewing staff and overseeing the progression of work from start to finish; I get to manage people and workflow, and I like that.

What do you dislike?

I definitely don't like the hours during peak season. I don't like the fact that I sometimes have to do the same thing over and over; for instance, if I have a client whose business has not changed much during a given year, it seems like I'm just doing the same tasks over and over again for the client. I didn't like the politics when I worked in a big firm—you definitely had to play the game to get the assignments you wanted—but now that I'm at a small firm, I don't have to deal with that anymore.

What is the biggest misconception about this job?

The biggest misconception is that accountants are completely numbers-oriented and have to have a fantastic GPA to have a good career. While that stuff is important, it's way more important to have good people skills to move ahead in your career. The outgoing person is going to have a more successful career than the person who locks himself up in his cubicle all day.

Looking back on your career or job search, what do you wish you had done differently?

I would have accepted a London assignment I was offered while I was at a big firm. That kind of experience would have been invaluable, especially in this era of globalization. And that kind of thing looks really good on your resume.

How can someone get a job like yours?

To people who are looking to start a career in accounting, I'd say attend campus visits by accounting firms. It's key to attend, even though the events can be a drag. Ask a lot of questions. These events can help you be sure you want a career in accounting, and they can help you get that first job. Just be aware that because they work in different areas for different firms, different people you talk to may give you different perspectives.

To people who are already in accounting, I'd say you have to work your network. Be aggressive. Keep up your relationships. Don't burn any bridges, because you will eventually encounter situations in which old contacts can help you. And you should also look into tax-specialist recruiters, who can be especially helpful if you're looking to change location geographically.

Describe a typical day.

10:00   I arrive at the office. Check e-mail, voice mail.

10:15   Start going through the stack of tax returns on my desk that have been prepared by my staff. Flag any questions or issues that I see in the returns.

11:30   Meet with my manager to discuss one client, the owner of a small business who seems to be using his business to pay personal expenses. We've been going back and forth on this one for a few weeks; the client wants to continue running personal expenses through his business and is willing to risk any penalties that might result, but we're unsure whether we're willing to sign his return; he may have to go elsewhere to get his taxes done.

12:30   Review more returns. Keep flagging issues and areas of concern.

1:30   Go out to lunch.

2:30   More tax returns to review.

3:30   E-mail a client, an individual who's being audited by the IRS. We need documentation for a number of investment transactions he made in the late 1990s, so I ask him to compile that documentation for us.

4:00   Get together with one of my staff to go over the tax returns I've reviewed so far today. Point out a number of technical mistakes that were made on the returns. This kind of as-we-go training is a significant part of the managerial aspect of my job.

5:30   Do some Internet research looking for cases and rulings that I want to find to support our position on some of our more aggressive clients' tax returns.

7:00   Finish up for the day and head home.

Director of Finance

Age: 38

Years in business: 14

Education: BS, accounting

Hours per week: 60 on average during tax season

Size of company: 80 employees

Certification: CPA, State of Arizona

Annual salary: $100,000 plus bonus

What do you do?

I work for an environmental consulting company. We do environmental compliance and planning work for companies, helping companies shepherd projects through the regulation process, with a focus on environmental issues. I'm the head of the finance team. I oversee everything from payroll to budgeting and forecasting. I oversee a staff of four.

How did you get your job?

I started my career as a staff accountant at a Big Five firm. Amazingly, I got my current job through Craig's List, a job-posting board. They were looking for an accountant who sounded fun. And I race cars and do ballet in addition to being an accountant. They called me in for an interview, so I researched the company and its industry and did all the things you're supposed to do before an interview, like come up with questions for the interviewer. I guess it worked, because I got the job.

What are your career aspirations?

I want to work my way up to the vice president of finance level. I don't think I want to become a CFO, because I'm too casual and low-key for that. I'd also like to get an MBA, because I'm one of the few people at this level in finance without an MBA, and it might be good for my career.

What kinds of people do well in this business?

You've got to be good analytically, of course. And you've got to have strong technical skills. You need to have an expert understanding of anything that has dollar signs attached to it, to understand your company's costs. For instance, I've got to understand Oracle enterprise software—how it works, how we're using it, what exactly we need. Beyond those things, you've got to have good people skills and communication skills, because you're working with people in different areas of the company. And the higher you go in accounting, the more important the soft-skills side of the equation becomes.

What do you really like about your job?

I love the fact that I have ultimate responsibility for the finances of the company. I like that I get to use my creativity; there are always different issues to look at in terms of the direction of the company, and I have to figure out how best to analyze those issues from a financial perspective and how to present those analyses. I like the fact that there are ever-changing needs—the business is constantly changing, so there are different issues I have to deal with every month. I like that I'm high enough on the food chain that I can influence the direction of the company, that my voice makes a difference in how the company is run. Finally, I like the fact that my decisions can benefit the company, by making it more financially sound, and the employees, by doing things like maximizing their benefits. For instance, recently, I saved our employees money on health insurance premiums by renegotiating with our insurance carrier.

What do you dislike?

I don't love the detail work, the number crunching. I don't like the fact that many people in business think they understand accounting and finance issues when in fact they really don't. Often it seems like people think they understand accounting and finance just because they know how to use Excel. I also don't enjoy the long hours. Having ultimate responsibility is a double-edged sword.

What is the biggest misconception about this job?

The biggest misconception is that accountants are all brainiacs with no social skills who just want to sit in a cubicle working on spreadsheets. That's absolutely not the case.

How can someone get a job like yours?

The first thing is to make sure you have enough tech skills to get a foot in the door in finance. Then, when you're in the early stages of your career, realize that you have to have 110 percent accuracy in your work as a young staff accountant. Finally, I think it's important to have outside interests—something to make you stand out from the crowd of nerds and white shirts. It worked for me; my current company looked at 500 resumes, but hired me because I had an interesting, well-rounded life.

Describe a typical day.

7:30   Get up, shower, and drink some coffee. Drive to work.

9:00   Arrive at the office.

9:15   Usually, when I arrive, there's some kind of emergency to take care of. Today our parent company needs to know who our top-ten customers were 2 years ago—ASAP. I look at archived e-mails and records and tell the VP who's looking for this information what he needs to know.

10:00   Meet with my staff to go over what they accomplished yesterday and what they're working on today. I love the fact that I don't have to crunch numbers as much as I used to—that I get to set the framework for what numbers need crunching and figure out what the numbers mean after they've been crunched, but don't have to do the dirty work that comes in between.

10:30   Deal with a couple of employees who are looking for information on vacation days and contractor payments.

11:00   Meet with an administrative manager and an IT manager about a couple of contracts with vendors. Decide I'll try to renegotiate our contracts with those vendors.

12:30 One of my team members sticks his head in my door before going to lunch, and I give him 5 bucks to pick up a salad for me. I eat lunch in the office 4 days a week on average.

1:30 Our East Coast office needs some financial reports from our office, so I put them together and e-mail them off while my East Coast colleagues are still at work.

2:00 Make a presentation to the company steering committee about the financial picture of the business.

3:00 Attend a meeting of the company's purchasing committee. We decide we should try to find a better deal on cell phones than the one we currently have. I analyze the proposal we're putting together, considering our cell phone usage and needs and the financial pros and cons of the various packages available.

5:00 This is when I get to really put my head down and get some work done—when most other people are on their way out of the office and things are getting quiet. I work on a project management schedule we're going to work against in the 10 days before the end of the quarter, when we'll have to present quarterly financial statements.

8:30 Finish up for the day and head home.

On the Job

The Workplace

- Lifestyle and Hours

- Culture

- Compensation

- Career Path

- Insider Scoop

Lifestyle and Hours

In accounting, the lifestyle and hours depend on your practice area, the time of year, the size of your firm, and your specific client or clients.

During the busy season (January to April), lower-level auditors can expect to work 55 to 60 or more hours per week; auditors at more senior levels may have to work even longer hours. During the rest of the year, auditors typically enjoy a standard 40-hour workweek.

Over in tax, the busy season depends on whether your client is a corporation (corporations have filing deadlines in March or September), an individual (April or October), or a partnership (April or October). Weekly hours during the busy season can range from 50 to 60 for staff to 70 to 80 for seniors. During the off-season, the pace cools to a steady 40 hours.

That said, the hours you work will depend largely on the clients to which you're assigned. Some clients may require you to put in longer hours and meet tighter deadlines. "This year I got killed during the busy season," says one insider who had a particularly demanding investment bank as a client.

Travel varies depending on your practice area and clients. Tax-compliance people spend nearly all their working time in their own office, while tax-consulting people can expect an occasional sojourn to the client's office. Audits take place at the client site, so local travel is quite common on the audit side. Those assigned to larger clients who have offices around the country may be required to travel more. If your client is based in New York but has a warehouse in the Midwest that needs to be inventoried, your team will probably be sent out to do the work. Employees who work in specialty practices may also travel longer distances because not all offices have specialty practices.

Culture

There are cultural variations between different firms, and between various offices of a given firm, and between firms of different size. In general, Big Four firms have a conservative, corporate atmosphere. These are mammoth firms, with all the hierarchical and bureaucratic implications their size implies. And these firms have Fortune 1000 clients. Taken together, all this means that professionalism is key to making it in these firms. Smaller firms can be more relaxed. Remember, though: No matter where you work, this is accounting—it's all about checking the numbers again and again. If you have an artistic personality, or are just plain disgusted by the thought of paperwork, accounting may not be the place for you. And that huge tattoo you're thinking of getting on your hand? It may help you get noticed by the opposite sex in biker bars, but it's not going to go over well with many of your clients—or your supervisor.

That's not to say that accountants don't know how to have fun. They do. Big Four firms are filled with work-hard/play-hard types just out of college, after all. "It's like freshman year all over again," says an insider. "You meet so many new people, and you're all in the same boat." Lower-level insiders say they go out a lot with their coworkers, and often hang out together on weekends. The big firms also sponsor sports teams, annual holiday parties, picnics, and other events.

There's more to all that socializing than having a good time, though. Networking plays a big role in accountants' client assignments and career paths, especially in the Big Four. One insider says, "Though you can skip the after-hours events, socializing and working yourself into the 'in' group is important because of the politics in staffing." In other words, there can be competition between you and your peers. In the near term, you're competing for plum client assignments. In the longer term, you're vying for a promotion to the next level in the corporate hierarchy—and because of firms' pyramid structure, there will be fewer jobs available at that next level than there will be people vying for those jobs.

Diversity

They say they've been working at fixing it, but a lack of ethnic diversity remains a problem at Big Four firms. Finding and retaining ethnic-minority employees is a difficult task for these firms, perhaps because of the paucity of minority senior-level people in the Big Four.

The story is better when it comes to gender diversity. The Big Four firms frequently make it onto the *Working Mother* list of the "100 Best Companies for Working Mothers," which takes into account job flexibility (e.g., telecommuting options), representation of women in companies, child care options, advancement opportunities for women (mentoring programs, support groups, and so on), how family-friendly companies' cultures are, and leave-program options for new parents.

Compensation

According to the U.S. Bureau of Labor Statistics, the median compensation for accountants of all kinds is about $47,000, and 80 percent of accountants earn between $30,320 and $82,730.

Entry-level employees in the Big Four generally earn in the mid $30,000s to low $40,000s. As you move up the seniority ladder, so will your compensation. As a senior, you'll make in the high $40,000s to low $60,000s. At the manager level, you'll make in the low $60,000s to low $80,000s. Partners generally make $120,000 or more, and senior partners can make $150,000 or more. Smaller-firm accountants may make a little less than their Big Four colleagues, depending on the firm and the clients. In general, those with advanced degrees earn around 10 percent more than others.

Accountants in industry are typically paid more than those at accounting firms, while those working in government typically earn a bit less. In the federal government, for example, junior accountants and auditors start at between $23,000 and $29,037, and those in nonsupervisory, supervisory and managerial positions average between $69,000 and $73,000.

After stagnating in the early 2000s, compensation for accountants of all kinds is on the rise. Raises won't generally be very big for those at the beginning of their accounting careers, but many senior level accountants are receiving raises in the 5 to 10 percent range in 2004.

The Workplace

Following are several compensation tables to give you a better idea of what industry and accounting firms are paying accountants of various types.

Certified Public Accountants

Level	Average Annual Salary ($)
Active owner of a CPA firm	150,371
More than 10 years' experience	71,224
6 to 10 years' experience	61,582
4 to 5 years' experience	50,662

Sources: 2003 PCPS/TSCPA National Management of the Accounting Practice Survey, PCPS, the American Institute of Certified Public Accountants' Alliance for CPA Firms, Jersey City, NJ, and the Texas Society of Certified Public Accountants, Dallas.

Corporate Finance and Accounting Professionals

Title	Average Annual Total Compensation ($)*
Chief financial officer	193,200
Treasurer	185,100
Vice president, finance	142,400
Assistant treasurer	130,200
Controller/comptroller	108,200
Cash manager	58,000

*Includes salary and bonus.
Source: AFP's 2003 Compensation Survey Report, Association for Finance Professionals, Bethesda, MD.

Corporate Accounting and Finance Executives

Title	Annual Company Sales ($M)	Salary Range ($)
Chief financial officer/treasurer*	500+	244,000–346,750
	250–500	170,750–230,750
	100–250	111,500–153,500
	50–100	92,750–122,500
	Up to 50	384,250–110,750
Vice president, finance*	500+	189,500–292,250
	250–500	150,000–225,750
	100–250	118,500–159,750
	50–100	95,000–125,000
	Up to 50	72,750–99,750
Director of finance	500+	120,750–178,750
	250–500	106,000–148,000
	100–250	88,250–124,000
	50–100	81,250–109,000
	Up to 50	80,000–89,000
Director of accounting	500+	115,500–157,250
	250–500	103,250–142,500
	100–250	83,250–114,500
	50–100	72,500–99,750
	Up to 50	64,750–90,250
Controller*	500+	104,250–145,750
	250–500	95,500–128,000
	100–250	80,500–107,250
	50–100	68,750–87,250
	Up to 50	61,250–73,500

Corporate Accounting and Finance Executives (cont'd)

Title	Annual Company Sales ($M)	Salary Range ($)
Assistant controller/assistant treasurer	500+	89,250–113,000
	250–500	77,750–97,000
	100–250	65,750–83,500
	50–100	56,500–72,500
	Up to 50	43,750–66,250
Tax director	500+	115,500–210,500
	250–500	86,000–128,750
Tax manager	500+	77,250–114,000
	250–500	64,000–85,000
Audit director	500+	120,000–200,000
	250–500	95,000–143,000
	100–250	79,750–115,250

*Bonuses and incentives reflect an increasingly large part of overall pay at this level and are not included in salary ranges. Graduate degrees and/or professional certifications are assumed at this level.

Note: Add up to 10 percent for graduate degrees or professional certifications.

Source: 2004 Salary Guide, Accountemps, Robert Half International Co., Menlo Park, CA.

Public Accountants in Audit, Tax, and Management Services

Title	Annual Salary Range ($)		
	Large*	Midsize*	Small*
Manager/director	77,750–119,000	68,000–93,750	63,750–84,500
Manager	63,000–82,250	57,000–74,250	52,000–66,000
Senior professional	48,750–62,250	44,000–56,500	41,000–54,000

*Large firms: $250 million in sales or more; midsize: $25 million to $250 million; small: up to $25 million.
Note: Add up to 10 percent for graduate degrees or professional certifications.
Source: 2004 Salary Guide, Accountemps, Robert Half International Co., Menlo Park, CA.

Vacation and Perks

Big Four hires generally start off with 3 weeks of vacation (or, alternately, 4 weeks of personal days, which cover both vacation days and sick days).

Big Four employees enjoy a host of benefits and perks, from 401(k) matching to child care to fitness clubs. Smaller-firm employees will probably not receive such luxurious perquisites.

Career Path

Most accounting-firm hires come in on the audit side. Generally, your first few years in public accounting are considered a kind of training period focused on your professional development, so that you can transition from a generalist/team-player role to a more specialized position with management responsibility—especially if, like most starting accountants, you go to a Big Four firm or one of the firms at the top of the second tier of accountancies.

The career path is fairly set in stone for Big Four employees. They enter their firms as staff accountants (or, in some firms, as assistant staff). After 2 or 3 years, they move to the senior accountant level. Two or 3 more years lead to the managing accountant level. With 8 or 10 years of experience, you become a senior manager. Finally, after 10, 12 or 14 years, you make partner.

Almost no one is skipped over for these regular promotions; if they are, a pink slip is usually on the way. Insiders report that there is usually a wave of staff that leaves the Big Four after a couple of years, when they have qualified for their CPAs, and then another wave that leaves after they get a year of management under their belt. If you perform extremely well, you can obtain early promotion.

In the Big Four, after your first couple of years or so on the audit side, you'll be required to specialize in a specific industry.

In corporate America, the career path generally starts at a junior accounting level, often in a specific accounting area, such as accounts receivable or controlling, and moves upward to manager, then to assistant controller or treasurer, then to director, then to vice president, then to CFO. It's more difficult to pin down the career path in industry than in public accounting, because different companies have different accounting needs and different available career paths.

CPAs who hang out their own shingles will find that their career path is basically what they make it, in terms of amount of work, income, areas of specialization, and types and sizes of clients.

The CPA designation is absolutely essential to moving up the ladder for many professionals in accounting and accounting-related careers, whether in public accounting firms, in the finance or accounting departments of corporations, government agencies, or other organizations, or among those who've hung out their own shingle. The requirements for becoming a Certified Public Accountant differ from state to state (check with your state's Board of Accountancy at www.nasba.org for more information). Most states require the completion of 150 hours of undergraduate-level coursework in accounting. Some states require a certain amount of professional experience. But no matter where you're located or would like to practice, to become a CPA, you've got to pass the CPA exam.

The New CPA Exam

Starting in late 2003, would-be CPAs stopped taking the old paper-based CPA exam administered by the AICPA (the American Institute of Certified Public Accountants) and started taking the new electronic version of the exam. The new exam is quite different from the old one, in terms of the exam's medium, the knowledge tested by the exam, and the schedule on which CPA candidates can take (and study for) the complete exam.

Basically, the new exam tests for knowledge that wasn't covered in the old test, knowledge of general business issues and information technology and an expanded set of candidate skills including the ability to analyze real-world cases, research skills, and communication skills. Candidates will have to complete tasks such as doing an electronic search for information in the Internal Revenue Code or writing a short business letter. In other words, way fewer multiple-choice questions.

In addition, the new exam is more flexible in terms of scheduling, and allows candidates to study for and take one section of the exam at a time, instead of requiring knowledge of all the exam's sections at once, in a single 2-day testing session.

To learn more about the new CPA exam—including what's on it, how and when to sign up for it, and how to prepare for it—and for practice exam content, visit www.cpa-exam.org. Candidates in each state will have to follow their state's application process and will receive their test scores from that state.

Side by Side: The Old CPA Exam vs. the New CPA Exam

What follows is a quick, side-by-side look at how the old paper exam and the new electronic exam stack up against each other.

Old CPA Exam vs. New CPA Exam

Paper Exam	Electronic Exam
Administered in May and November.	Different sections administered online at least 5 days a week in April and May, July and August, October and November, and January and February.
Whole exam taken in one 2-day session.	In most states, can be taken one part at a time, with 18 months to pass all four parts of the exam once the first exam part is passed (but can only take the same exam section once in a single testing window).
Consists of three parts: Auditing & Attestation, Financial Accounting & Reporting, and Regulation.	Consists of four parts: Auditing & Attestation, Financial Accounting & Reporting, Regulation, and a new exam section called Business Environment & Concepts. The new section tests knowledge, previously untested by the CPA exam, of topics such as economics, finance, forecasting and financial planning, and information technology.
15½ hours long.	14 hours long.
Lots and lots of multiple-choice questions.	Includes real-world cases, and tests new skills such as case analysis, electronic research ability, and communication ability.
Based more on memorization of accounting principles and rules.	Based on a more analytical and "real world" approach to solving problems.

Insider Scoop

What's Great about Accounting

Big Four Jobs = Resume Gold

Let's face it. Big Four accounting firms' retention rates are low for a reason: These jobs make great stepping-stones. Insiders say their exposure to a wide range of companies and industries and the vast responsibility given to them allows them to develop impressive skill sets, whether they want to hang out their own accounting shingle, go into finance in industry, or go into another profession entirely. One insider says, "When I look back on my 4 years, what I've learned is unbelievable. In college, it would have taken me 10 years to learn this much."

Big Four = Cutting-Edge Technology

Big Four firms are renowned for their early adoption of technology. One insider says, "I take a lot of it for granted, but we really have an unreal amount of information at our fingertips. The intranet, external Web, the research capabilities—it's almost information overload at times."

Stability

Despite the fact that Andersen has fallen flat on its face, forcing thousands of people to scramble to find new employers, the accounting industry remains a bastion of stability. After all, in good times and bad, corporations and other institutions need accountants. And the career path remains pretty set in stone. Assuming you can do the work and do it well and are willing to put in a few extra hours when necessary, you can fairly accurately predict where you'll be in 5, 10, or even 15 years.

It's the People

Many young accountants in big firms enjoy the fact that they're surrounded by other folks who are a lot like them: young, college-educated, and up for going out and socializing with coworkers. One insider says, "It's great in the Big Four. The people are smart—they all graduated with good GPAs from good schools—and they're fun."

What's Not So Great about Accounting

Big Four Politics

Internal politics play a big role when it comes to staffing at the Big Four. Why? Everyone wants to get put on good, visible projects that can help them advance up the career ladder. An insider says, "Your success depends on what kinds of clients you get put on. If you get put on clients that are a total mess, it changes the whole ballgame; you're working lots of overtime and are under a lot of pressure. Conversely, if you're put on a good project and the partner likes you, you have a chance to show your stuff. All this depends on whom you rub elbows with."

Big = Bureaucracy

The Big Four are mammoth companies, and some insiders say that they feel overwhelmed by their size at times. According to one, "If you're not used to a big corporate atmosphere, it can come as kind of a shock. You go to office-wide meetings where you see people you've never seen before and will probably never see again." And bureaucracy is a natural offshoot of these firms' size and business focus. Accounting involves myriad rules, regulations, reviews, and checklists, and some insiders say that a feeling of administration overload creeps unnecessarily into other aspects of their professional lives. One insider says, "I'm really busy, and it just seems like a lot of the administration stuff isn't really necessary." If you dread red tape, beware!

The Hours

Especially during tax season, accountants are notorious for working late. There are always client demands to be met and numbers to be checked—and double-checked. During busy season, accountants can expect to work 55-hour weeks, and depending on the client, may be required to work 60- or 70-hour weeks. Be prepared to do what it takes to get the work done—even if it means sacrificing your personal life. One insider says of a particularly grueling assignment, "I didn't see anyone for 3 months. I became a social loser." For some in the industry, the travel can be a drain, too. An insider says, "A lot of people get sick of going from client to client, especially as they grow older."

Not Rocket Science

Several insiders use the phrase "it's just accounting" when describing their line of work. While accounting does offer more flexibility and variety than most people think, you won't be asked to reinvent the wheel or build a better mousetrap. A large portion of the work involves checking to make sure that numbers conform to the Generally Accepted Accounting Principles (GAAP). If you long to create and innovate, accounting is probably not the ideal place for you.

Lack of Diversity at the Top

While Big Four accounting firms recruit a very diverse crowd for their entry-level positions, at least in terms of race and gender, at the end of the long, hard slog to the partner level, it's usually white males who are still in the race. If being a partner in a Big Four firm is your career goal, *caveat emptor*.

The Pay

While an accounting career can provide a comfortable lifestyle, this is probably not a career that's going to make you truly rich, especially not at a young age. Which can make for pangs of jealousy when accountants rub shoulders with folks like investment bankers and lawyers, whose job descriptions can have a lot of overlap with those of accountants. One Big Four insider says, "I know a lot of attorneys. I know what they do on the job, what they have to know to do their job, the scope of their responsibilities, and how much education they had to have to get where they are. And I think accountants are underpaid."

Getting Hired

- Who Does Well

- The Recruiting Process

- Interviewing Tips

- Getting Grilled

- Grilling Your Interviewer

Who Does Well

Finance and accounting jobs require critical, detail-oriented thinking. If you have a knack for using numbers to understand patterns that influence business, you're going to be valuable to a company. If you can't crunch and analyze them, this isn't going to be the right job for you. You should also like, and be good at, solving problems and be able to think critically about the numbers you're working with.

While accountants need to be good at math and have strong analytical-thinking and research skills, attention to detail is usually considered more important. And to develop business relationships and close new business, accounting professionals find it necessary to develop strong written and verbal communication skills.

The American Institute of Certified Public Accountants (AICPA) strongly recommends that all accountants balance their technical business training with a classically liberal education. Furthermore, as business is increasingly being performed electronically, accountants need to pick up as much knowledge about computers and information systems as possible, not only to understand their utility but also to assess their value to clients.

Requirements

The vast majority of accounting jobs require at least a bachelor's degree from a 4-year university. In fact, according to the AICPA, within the next few years, 48 states will require 150 hours of university education—30 hours more than for a regular 4-year degree—before you can even take the test to become a CPA. Currently, more than 40 states have adopted the 150-hour requirement, while the remaining states/jurisdictions continue to work toward adoption.

While college is almost always a requirement, what you can study is beginning to broaden tremendously. With the rise of accounting software that's now taking care of much book balancing, accounting firms are looking to business and finance majors to work in accounting departments. Degrees in finance, business, and even management of information systems (MIS) are definitely good things to have when trying to land a job as a management accountant or internal auditor.

And once that bachelor's degree is out of the way, most accountants who go on to get their Master's degree don't get a Master's of Accounting (MA). Much more popular are MBAs with a specialization in either finance or accounting. And again, any education you pick up relating to technology and information systems is going to be a big ace to carry around in your pocket.

Once you have school out of the way, the next step for many accountants is getting licensed. To become a CPA, even after 150 hours of undergraduate courses, in many states you need to work for about a year before you can take the exam.

Even for accounting jobs that don't require a CPA—such as internal auditing and management accounting—there are organizations that provide certification, such as the Institute of Internal Auditors or the Institute of Management Accountants. Although the government does not regulate certification by these groups, many employers are starting to require such certification anyway, and having it can open many doors for you.

Perhaps the only exception to the need for a formal education and getting licensed are the accounting positions that fall under the category of bookkeeping. Here, there are many openings for people straight out of high school, those who have 2-year degrees from technical colleges, or those who have 4-year degrees in unrelated or nonbusiness areas. As always, there's a trade-off: With less school, expect less pay and much less stimulating work.

The Recruiting Process

The good news here is that accounting firms are hiring. Between things like new accounting rules and increasing mergers and acquisitions activity, public accountancies are staffing up. Because of these things and a few others, management accountants, who work in-house for companies of all kinds, are also finding increasing opportunities.

Undergrads and Accounting Grad Students

The Big Four recruit on campus at undergrad and grad schools across the country, and many firms in the second tier recruit on campus, as well (though there is a more regional focus at many of these firms). Firms that recruit on campus typically provide campus presentations—it's a good idea to attend these to start learning about the major firms. The interviewing process begins with first-round on-campus interviews. After the initial round of interviews, recruiters will choose candidates to be called back for second-round interviews. Some firms conduct one or two big office interviewing days for the second round; others spread the office visits out.

Students at campuses where the firm of their choice doesn't have a presence should contact the company directly. Remember: The best way to make this M.O. work is to network and find a personal contact within the firm of your choice.

Midcareer Candidates

It's a good time to be an experienced accountant on the lookout for a new job. With the workload picking up due to new accounting rules and increasing M&A activity in industry, public accounting firms are keen to hire experienced professionals who can come in and add value immediately. And as business picks up across industries, look for in-house finance and accounting opportunities to grow as well.

The best way to find a new job as an experienced candidate is to work your industry contacts. Get in touch with the people you went to school with. Get in touch with people you used to work with. Contact other members of professional organizations you belong to. Consider joining new professional organizations to increase your network. And so on.

Interviewing Tips

1. **Dress the part.** Accounting firms are rule-bound institutions (especially the Big Four); conservative attire is a must for the interview. Think Brooks Brothers, not Versace.

2. **Take time to prepare** for the interview. Research the firm—online, for instance, or by attending campus information sessions. Know what makes it different from its competitors and what makes you a perfect fit.

3. **Don't lie.** If a recruiter asks for experience you don't have, don't make something up. In the long run, your honesty will do more for you than even the cleverest lie (especially given the greater emphasis placed on ethics in accounting these days).

4. **Listen carefully** to the questions the interviewer asks, and **make sure you're responding to the questions asked.**

6. **Know (and be able to communicate) why you would make a good accountant.**

7. **Think through your experience;** you should have at the ready stories that display attributes like your

   - Analytical ability.
   - Teamwork skills.
   - Leadership skills.
   - Communication skills.
   - Problem-solving skills.
   - Ability to work independently.
   - Integrity.
   - Proficiency with technology.

8. **Have questions prepared** to ask your interviewer—preferably questions whose answers you'd truly like to know. Some areas around which to frame your questions include:

   - Training opportunities
   - Interaction between the lower ranks and senior managers and partners
   - The overall firm culture, as well as possible cultural differences between different offices
   - What actions the firm takes to retain and motivate employees
   - How much of a say you'll have over which assignments you'll get
   - Differences between the firm and its competitors
   - Bigger-picture questions about the state of the industry after the fall of Andersen and the de-linkage of accounting and consulting (which will show your knowledge of and passion for the industry)

9. **Be positive.** While you may be interested in knowing more about the firm's recent ethical and business gaffes, it's probably a better idea to focus on more positive topics in the interview. If you come across as someone who believes that accountants are evil and accounting is not a noble profession, you won't get hired.

10. **Don't focus on compensation** in your interviews. Doing so tells your interviewer that you're more interested in what you'll be making than in what you'll be doing with your life.

11. **Don't whine about previous managers or employers.** Doing so can raise questions about your ability to take orders and work as part of a team.

Getting Grilled

Some interviewers work from a script, others wing it, and still others tailor their questions to your particular background. Here are some things they might ask:

- What excites you most about a career in accounting?

- What do you want your career to look like in 5 years? 10 years?

- What makes you want to work for this accountancy rather than for our competitors?

- Tell me about your leadership experience.

- Tell me about a time when you were faced with a problem that was difficult to solve. What was the problem? What steps did you take to solve it? How was the situation resolved?

- Tell me about a time you were faced with a dilemma—a difficult decision with no obvious "correct" course of action. How did you decide to make the decision you ultimately made?

- Tell me about a time when you worked together with a team. What was the team trying to do? What was your role within the team? Was the team successful in achieving its goals?

- What other firms are you interviewing with?

Grilling Your Interviewer

This is your chance to turn the tables and find out what you want to know. We strongly encourage you to spend time preparing questions of your own. In the meantime, the samples below should get you started. The "Rare" questions are meant to be boring and innocuous, while the "Well Done" ones will help you put the fire to your interviewer's feet.

Rare

- What are the training/mentoring opportunities I will receive at [name of firm]?

- How successful have [name of firm]'s efforts to improve retention rates been?

- How much interaction will I have with senior managers and partners?

- How are knowledge-management advances changing the way [name of firm] serves its clients?

Medium

- How technical will my skill set need to be?

- Why should a client choose [name of firm] over one of its competitors?

- If you could change three things about [name of firm], what would they be?

- What are the differences you've noticed between the cultures at various [name of firm] offices, and what is the culture like at the office I would be assigned to?

- How much of a say will I have in the types of engagements I will be working on in my first 2 years?

Well Done

- How have the corporate accounting scandals changed the way the firm attracts new business?

- Has [name of firm] taken any specific steps to instill a sense of the importance of ethics in early-career accountants?

- Are there politics involved in how work assignments are made at [name of firm]?

- How diverse is the workforce at [name of firm]? Are the firm's efforts to improve diversity working?

For Your Reference

- Industry Glossary

- Recommended Reading

- Online Resources

Industry Glossary

10-K. An audited annual report of a U.S. public company's financial and business condition. Required of public companies by the Securities and Exchange Commission (SEC).

10-Q. A nonaudited quarterly report of a U.S. public company's financial and business condition. Required of public companies by the SEC.

Accrual basis. An accounting method that recognizes revenues when they are earned, rather than when they're received, and costs when they are incurred, rather than when they're paid. Compare to "cash basis."

Active asset. An asset used by a company in its regular operations. For instance, for a construction company, a cement truck might be an active asset.

Balance sheet. Financial statement showing a company's assets, liabilities, and equity.

Book value. The value of an asset as recorded in a company's financial statements; can differ by quite a lot from the asset's actual value in the marketplace.

Burn rate. The net amount of money a company is spending in a given period (e.g., monthly or annual burn rate). Used to help evaluate how long a company that has not reached profitability can survive given the amount of money it has in the bank.

Capex. Short for capital expense. An expense incurred to acquire or upgrade a physical asset such as a warehouse or a computer system.

Capitalize. To recognize a cost over time, rather than as a single expense against current operations.

Carrying cost. The cost of holding inventory.

Cash basis. An accounting method that recognizes revenues when they are received, rather than when they're earned, and costs when they are paid, rather than when they're incurred. Compare to "accrual basis."

Clean opinion. A public accountant's full endorsement of a client company's accounting of its financial condition. Also known as an *unqualified opinion.* Compare to "qualified opinion."

Comptroller. A company's head accountant. Also known as a *controller.*

Consolidated financial statement. A financial statement representing the combined financial state of a holding company's various businesses.

Cooked books. Financial statements that fraudulently misrepresent a company's financial condition.

Cookie-jar accounting. A method of accounting that allows a company to make its financial performance seem more consistent than it actually is. Involves taking reserves against losses in years of better performance and using those reserves to offset poorer performance in other years.

Current asset. An asset that is expected to be liquidated or used up within a single accounting cycle or calendar year. For example, a ton of feed grain might be considered a current asset on a livestock farm's books.

Differential accounting. Using two different accounting standards, one for public companies and one for private companies.

Environmental accounting. Accounting specialty that focuses on the environmental issues facing a company. May participate in environmental compliance audits and/or manage or prevent claims due to environmental issues.

Forensic accounting. Accounting specialty that focuses on ferreting out accounting fraud and financial malfeasance.

GAAP. Short for Generally Accepted Accounting Principles. The commonly accepted rules for proper accounting, as recognized by the Financial Accounting Standards Board (FASB).

Income statement. Financial statement representing revenues and costs during a given period.

Off-balance-sheet transaction. A transaction that may affect a company's financial condition but does not appear on its balance sheet. For instance, while the receipt of financing via the issuance of debt or equity offerings would appear on a company's balance sheet, the company may receive off-balance-sheet financing via joint ventures or partnerships.

Qualified opinion. A public accountant's statement of agreement with the accuracy of a company's financial statements with one or more caveats. An accountant may give a qualified opinion to a client's financial statements due to having insufficient information about an item or items in the statements or because of a future event that may or may not occur. For example, an accountant may give a qualified opinion of a radio broadcasting company's financial statements because the statements assume that the company will renew its contract to broadcast the games of a professional sports team and thus earn higher advertising revenue than it might with its normal all-news format.

Top line. A company's total revenue in a given period.

Working capital. Current assets minus current liabilities. Shows how much a company has in the way of net liquid assets.

Write down. To lower the value of an asset on a company's books.

Recommended Reading

Accountant's Guide to Fraud Detection and Control

Howard R. Davia et al. (John Wiley & Sons, 2000).
A look at the ins and outs of how corporate accounting fraud happens, and how it can be prevented. Certainly of interest to those considering forensic accounting careers.

Building Public Trust: The Future of Corporate Reporting

Samuel A. DiPiazza and Robert G. Eccles (John Wiley & Sons, 2002).
This book, coauthored by the CEO of PricewaterhouseCoopers, presents a framework for transparent, effective financial reporting.

Corporate Finance

Stephen A. Ross, Randolph W. Westerfield, and Jeffrey Jaffe (McGraw-Hill, 2002).
A detailed picture of how corporate finance works. Covers a host of core financial concepts including equity valuation, options theory, risk, bond math, and financial analysis.

Final Accounting: Ambition, Greed and the Fall of Arthur Andersen

Barbara Ley Toffler and Jennifer Reingold (Broadway Books, 2003).
Written by the person who ran Andersen's business ethics practice, this book chronicles how a culture of looking the other way when there was money to be made resulted in the fall of a once-mighty accounting firm.

Getting Started in Financial Consulting

Edward Stone (John Wiley & Sons, 2000).
How to start your own financial counseling business, including financial management theory and practice, marketing ideas to grow your business, a review of
certification programs, and so on.

Getting Started in Tax Consulting

Gary Carter (John Wiley & Sons, 2001).
A good resource for would-be tax return-preparers/consultants, this book
includes strategies for breaking into and building your own business.

Internal Control: A Manager's Journey

K. H. Spencer Pickett (John Wiley & Sons, 2001).
A look at how to design, document, implement, and manage internal control
policies to maximize accountability and control risk.

Managing the Professional Service Firm

David Maister (Free Press, 1997).
A study of the structures and practices of well-run professional services firms,
looking at things like the management of growth, the generation of new business, ongoing client relationships, training, time management, the delegation of
work and the autonomy of employees, and compensation programs. Might be
worth a look to help evaluate whether the firms you're considering are well run.

The Financial Numbers Game: Detecting Creative Accounting Practices

Charles Mulford and Eugene Comiskey (John Wiley & Sons, 2002).
Considers the effect of technology, competition, consolidation, the erosion of
public trust, and low employee morale on the accounting profession, and talks
about innovative paths to excellence for firms dealing with those and other factors.

The Firm of the Future:
A Guide for Accountants, Lawyers, and Other Professional Services

Paul Dunn and Ronald Baker (John Wiley & Sons, 2003).

Deconstructs the dynamic forces at work in the accounting world of the 21st century—things like new technology, intense competition, consolidation, the erosion of public trust, and many other challenges.

The Number: How the Drive for Quarterly Earnings Corrupted
Wall Street and Corporate America

Alex Berenson (Random House, 2003).

Details the business and market conditions that resulted in the current era of corporate scandals. These conditions are what the accounting industry was up against as it tried and failed to avoid the temptation of facilitating corporate accounting misdeeds.

Unaccountable: How the Accounting Profession Forfeited a Public Trust

Mike Brewster (John Wiley & Sons, 2003).

Traces the history of the accounting industry from the days when it was dominated by the Big Eight to today's post-Enron Big Four era.

Online Resources

- The American Institute of Certified Public Accountants (www.aicpa.org/index.htm) offers a plethora of accounting news and information.

- AccountingWEB (www.accountingweb.com) is a great source for news and resources for would-be accountants.

- *The Next Generation Accountant* research guide, available from Robert Half International Inc. and containing information about the directions accounting is headed in, is available for download at www.nextgenaccountant.com/research_hili/research_guide.html. And it's free.

- The American Institute of Certified Public Accountants (AICPA) site (www.aicpa.org/pubs/cpaltr/jan2003/supps/large5.htm) includes an article on 2003 trends in accounting compensation. (Hint: Compensation is going up!)

- The AICPA site also has a page full of links to information about the Sarbanes-Oxley Act: www.aicpa.org/sarbanes/index.asp.

- *Forbes* has an interesting series of articles titled "Watching the Books," looking at the top areas of interest in accounting currently, including pensions, stock options, off-balance-sheet corporate activity, capitalized costs, and real earnings. Available at www.forbes.com/2003/02/04/cz_em_0131acctland.html.

- The AICPA Career Center website (www.cpa2biz.com/Career/default.htm) includes a self-assessment tool, a salary guide, accounting job postings, and articles on the job search and other accounting career issues.

- Beta Alpha Psi (www.bap.org) is an accounting and business fraternity organization connecting accounting students, academics, and professionals.

- The National Association of Black Accountants (www.nabainc.org) is a resource for African Americans and other minorities in accounting.

- The Association of Certified Fraud Examiners (www.cfenet.com/home.asp) has resources for those who are CFEs or wish to become CFEs.

- WebCPA (www.webcpa.com) offers a range of news and columns on current issues relating to accounting.

- The Uniform CPA Examination website (www.cpa-exam.org) hosts learning resources, including a tutorial, to help people preparing for the exam.

WETFEET'S INSIDER GUIDE SERIES

JOB SEARCH GUIDES

Getting Your Ideal Internship

Job Hunting A to Z: Landing the Job You Want

Killer Consulting Resumes

Killer Investment Banking Resumes

Killer Resumes & Cover Letters

Negotiating Your Salary & Perks

Networking Works!

INTERVIEW GUIDES

Ace Your Case: Consulting Interviews

Ace Your Case II: 15 More Consulting Cases

Ace Your Case III: Practice Makes Perfect

Ace Your Case IV: The Latest & Greatest

Ace Your Case V: Return to the Case Interview

Ace Your Interview!

Beat the Street: Investment Banking Interviews

Beat the Street II: I-Banking Interview Practice Guide

CAREER & INDUSTRY GUIDES

Careers in Accounting

Careers in Advertising & Public Relations

Careers in Asset Management & Retail Brokerage

Careers in Biotech & Pharmaceuticals

Careers in Brand Management

Careers in Consumer Products

Careers in Entertainment & Sports

Careers in Human Resources

COMPANY GUIDES